THE TATE GALLERY

THE
TATE GALLERY

BY

JOHN ROTHENSTEIN

Director, The Tate Gallery

HARRY N. ABRAMS, INC · PUBLISHERS · NEW YORK

LIBRARY OF CONGRESS CATALOG CARD NUMBER: 63-12768
1963
PRINTED IN WEST GERMANY BY CARL SCHÜNEMANN
THIS BOOK IS PUBLISHED IN FRANCE BY
EDITIONS AIMERY SOMOGY, PARIS

CONTENTS

FOREWORD

For my sketch of the Tate Gallery's history the primary sources are the minutes of the Meetings of the Trustees of the National and Tate Galleries and the Reports of the several Committees that have been convened to consider the affairs of the National Collections, the correspondence of the National and Tate Galleries, and newspaper cuttings. These sources I have referred to in my narrative as occasion required. It should be added, however, that between the opening years of this century and 1938 virtually no press cuttings were preserved at the Tate; between 1930 and 1938 and occasionally earlier there are gaps in the Gallery's correspondence.

I must record my thanks to Miss Corinne Bellow for assistance given in what otherwise would have been her leisure hours.

Newington, Oxfordshire, 1962   JOHN ROTHENSTEIN

THE CONCEPTION

Throughout the nineteenth century there was in England growing disquiet over the inadequacy of the representation of the British School of painting in the national collection. The National Gallery, established in 1824, had quickly won a place among the great galleries of the world. The judgment and enterprise of successive Directors, and the initiative allowed them, backed by funds which in terms of today's purchasing power were considerable, assembled within a few decades outstanding collections of Italian, Dutch and Flemish paintings and a Spanish collection which, although less complete, included paintings of high distinction. It can hardly be questioned that in concentrating upon the building-up of as complete a representation as possible of the great painting of Europe the National Gallery acted with wisdom. Masterpieces were secured at a time when rivalry was slight; in the competitive later years of the century and after, they would surely have eluded the British official collector. The representation of British painting at the National Gallery was by comparison haphazard and uneven. It included fine examples of the work of a number of the principal masters, but a larger number of those of men of insignificant stature: Callcott, Howard, Thompson, Herbert, Cooke, Simpson, Sleap and Halls, are names, for instance, that surprisingly by present standards, figure in the National Gallery catalogue of 1890.

However necessary the relative neglect of the native in favour of foreign schools, the dissatisfaction of native artists and other interested persons was not surprising. The power and wealth of Great Britain and her manifold activity and inventiveness had given her a position of eminence in the world such as she had never before enjoyed, even in the times of the first Elizabeth and the elder Pitt. The suggestion, implicit in her meagre and incoherent representation in Trafalgar Square, that she was inferior in one of the most brilliant fields of human endeavour was therefore unpalatable. This dissatisfaction, however, sprang from something besides national pride, namely the well-founded conviction that the countrymen of Chaucer, Spenser, Shakespeare, Milton, Dryden and Wordsworth had also painted pictures which were not unworthy of admiration. It was remembered that Constable and Bonington had been celebrated in France; that Lawrence had been acclaimed as the most illustrious portrait painter of his time, and that the most eloquent pen that had ever written about painting had proclaimed the supreme genius of Turner. Ruskin, although the principal subjects of his writings were drawn from the past, was one of those to whom study was never an end but always a means of elevating the mind, of relieving the lot of man. Commenting on his aims as Slade Professor he wrote that 'their primary business, and mine, was with art in Oxford now; not with art in Florence then'. He did indeed go on to say that this business could not be settled until the prior question was settled, namely 'Why have our little girls large shoes?' One of the principal effects of his writings, however remote their subjects in time, was ever to direct the mind of his readers – that is to say, almost the whole of literate England – towards the present. Moreover he wrote about contemporaries, sometimes severely, but sometimes with exalted hopefulness. Championing the young Pre-Raphaelites he held out the hope that they might 'lay in our England the foundations of a school of art nobler than the world has seen for three hundred years'. [1] Responsible men, thanks largely to Ruskin, perceived something of the function of the arts, in a great civilization, of awakening and guiding the highest imagination.

As decade succeeded decade dissatisfaction with the public representation of British art grew more insistent, and various measures of improvement were taken. The first was the bequest, in 1840, by the successful sculptor Sir Francis Chantrey, of his large fortune for the purchase, as stated in his Will, of 'Works of Fine Art, of the highest merit that can be obtained, either already executed, or which may hereafter be executed by artists of any nation, provided such artists shall have actually resided in Great Britain during the executing and completing of such works.' An interesting feature of this enlightened bequest is that it had among its aims the establishment of a separate national collection of British art. Between the time when the Chantrey Bequest was established and when it came into effect in 1876 after Lady Chantrey's death, three collections – one of the utmost importance – were presented or bequeathed to the nation's existing collections of British pictures: the Robert Vernon Gift, made in 1847, of 157 paintings and a group of sculpture; the Turner Bequest, through which the National Gallery became possessed in 1856 of 282 oil paintings and over 19,000 water-colours, and the Sheepshanks Gift, in 1857, of 233 British paintings, which was made specifically to the Victoria and Albert Museum.

These benefactions brought a number of examples of art of the highest quality into the national possession, yet their effect, so far from placating opinion critical of the public representation of British art, served to intensify it. The Sheepshanks pictures were at South Kensington, where the Chantrey purchases were also housed, and the Turner Bequest and the Vernon Gift were housed but largely unshown in the overcrowded National Gallery. The collection of British art in national possession was in fact scattered, miscellaneous, and difficult to see.

In the spring of 1890 two disconnected events touched off into a blaze this long-smouldering discontent. On 10th March reports appeared in several newspapers that Mr Henry Tate of Streatham had offered to present about sixty of his modern English pictures, valued at about £90,000, to the Trustees of the National Gallery, subject to their being housed without unnecessary delay in Trafalgar Square. Two days later the landscape painter James Orrock – an ardent though sometimes injudicious advocate of British art – read a paper in the rooms of the Society of Arts in which he made a plea for the fuller representation of the British School at the National Gallery. *The Times*, which appears to have been aware of Tate's communication to the National Gallery, written on 23rd October 1889, irked, no doubt, by the premature disclosure of the substance of it, and fully sharing the dissatisfaction voiced by Orrock, published on 13th March a closely reasoned and eloquent leading article in his support. In one crucial particular it adopted a far more radical standpoint. Orrock was concerned with the overcrowded and constricted Trafalgar Square; *The Times* demanded 'a really representative and choice collection of our art gathered together in some great central gallery ... a gallery that shall do for English art what the Luxembourg does for French', and flatly declared that 'the time has come for the creation of a great British Gallery'.

Tate's offer resulted, in the course of the two and a half ensuing years, in the consideration, to the accompaniment of furious controversy, of a succession of sites for the 'British Luxembourg' – the project itself rallied ardent and ever-increasing support – but these proved either to be unavailable or else unacceptable to Tate. (J. C. Robinson had weightily urged, for instance, the building of a new British gallery on a site adjacent to Kensington Palace.)[2]

It became evident before long that the National Gallery found the acceptance of Tate's offer a matter of difficulty, and he accordingly made public[3] a further offer addressed to the Chancellor of the Exchequer, J. G. Goschen, that he had also made privately to the Trustees,[4] namely that the Government should sanction the establishment of a national gallery exclusively confined to works by British artists, to which he would be prepared to present fifty-seven pictures which he listed and any others in his possession. To this offer he attached several proposals, the chief of which was that the new foundation should be placed 'under a distinctly separate administration from that of any existing institution'. Another proposal – which acquits Tate of the charge, nevertheless often repeated, of aiming at the establishment of a public gallery solely to house his own pictures – was that in order that the representation of British art should be as complete as possible the transfer to the new institution should be considered of the works of British artists at the National Gallery and at South Kensington. Tate's offer was warmly welcomed by *The Times* as bringing forward in concrete form the question of a British gallery. 'Everyone agrees, in fact,' ran its leading article, 'that we ought to have such a gallery....'[5] *The Daily News* was not less cordial in

12

support: 'The great value of Mr Tate's proposition ... is in its suggestiveness. His scheme ... is a great one', but, it warned, 'it would have to be administered on principles of knowledge and devotion that would compel the rejection of a part of his generous offer from his own store.' Four days later *The Times* published the Treasury's reply, which offered for the purpose urged by Tate two tunnel-like structures in South Kensington known as the 'Eastern' and 'Western' Galleries – a proposal which originated in a memorandum drawn up by Lord Carlisle and accepted by his fellow Trustees of the National Gallery.

The effect of Tate's new offer and of the Government's response to it was still further to heighten public interest. Numerous articles appeared in the press throughout the country, and considering that where the arts are concerned differences of opinion are inevitable there was a rare degree of agreement about the desirability of Tate's project and the unsuitability of the proffered accommodation. 'The Democracy', wrote *Reynolds News*, 'are interested in the establishment of a National Gallery of British Art.'[7] 'The English Luxembourg must at once spring into existence', was the opinion of *Land and Water*,[8] and it was the view of *The Huddersfield Chronicle* 'that there ought no longer to be any doubt about its establishment'.[9]

In a leading article *The Times* described the use of 'the long, cheerless corridors' at South Kensington as being 'very far from the ideal solution'.[10] In two long letters[11] published in *The Times*, Harry Quilter, the art critic, gave effective support to the idea of such a gallery as Tate envisaged, and offered to contribute £2,000 towards its establishment and maintenance. In the second of these is made, possibly for the first time, a recommendation with regard to purchasing which, after the passage of many years, became a special feature of Tate Gallery policy, namely that low-priced works should be purchased from the younger artists. 'By so doing', he observes, the gallery authorities no doubt 'will make frequent mistakes, and will, as far as my experience goes, encounter both ingratitude and even opposition from those whom they wish to serve; but they will inevitably afford much valuable encouragement to the worthier members of the craft'. The projected gallery also found an influential supporter in William Agnew, who offered to contribute £10,000 provided that the Kensington Palace site was selected.[12]

A statement made by Lord Cranbrook on behalf of the Government emphasized that it was favourable to the principle of a fully representative gallery of British art under independent administration, but that it proposed to adapt the 'Eastern' and 'Western' Galleries for its accommodation.[13]

There was a further development the following spring when Humphry Ward made public[14] some correspondence that had passed between the Chancellor of the Exchequer and himself regarding the offer, on the part of a friend who desired that his name should not be made public, to defray the cost of building a gallery upon a plot of vacant land fronting Imperial Institute Road. In the course of it, although he gave no specific undertaking about the plot of land proposed, the Chancellor suggested that Ward's friend 'should rely upon the obvious obligations' of the Government; Ward's friend accordingly declared himself happy to regard the Chancellor's letter as an acceptance on the part of the Government of his offer.

The anonymous friend was generally, and correctly, presumed to be Tate.

There was strong opposition on the part of scientific interests to the intrusion of an art gallery into part of a site which they understood to have been set aside for a new Science Museum. This opposition eventually proved effective, and attempts were made to secure a site near the Temple on the Embankment, but its owners, the Corporation of London, put so high a price upon it that the project had to be abandoned. The Chancellor offered a smaller site in South Kensington and again commended the rejected 'Eastern' and 'Western' Galleries. Tate withdrew his offer, observing that the site denied him under pressure from scientific interests was one which the Government itself had proposed.[15]

Tate's withdrawal provoked an outcry. His project had raised determined opposition: he had been accused of desiring to advertise sugar, and his offer described as the £80,000 bribe of the sugar-

14

boiler.[16] So unjust were the attacks that *The Speaker* was moved to print an article in his defence entitled 'Are "Benefactors" Malefactors?'[17] But reference to the contemporary press in general suggests that the failure of the attempts of a generous and a patient man to give to the nation something of which it stood in manifest need was widely regretted. *Punch* published a rondeau entitled 'Entêtement Britannique', which read, in part:

> Yet gifts are treated with disdain,
> Which gives the would-be donors pain—
> We've got a name to call *that* by,
> *Mal à la* TATE.[18]

In the same journal's 'Essence of Parliament' the Minister concerned is accused of 'making Tate out as a cantankerous wrong-headed person who, proposing to bestow £160,000 in the way of a free gift, expected to have his wishes consulted. . . .'[19]

The serious opposition to the proffered gallery, although it involved unkind references to Tate in the press, sprang neither from personal unfriendliness to the man nor from doubts about the eventual desirability of a gallery for British art. Its motive was the fear that such a gallery might become a stronghold of the Royal Academy.

After the disintegration of the Pre-Raphaelite movement in the 'fifties, British art had entered the dreariest epoch of its history. The official art world – entirely dominated by the Royal Academy – was in its complacency as indifferent to the great examples set by Constable and Turner as to the patient ardour of the Pre-Raphaelites, hostile to Whistler and – as far as it was aware of it – to Impressionism, which was winning recognition in France and in the United States. Pomposity, triviality, dullness and self-satisfaction were the order of the day. There existed, nevertheless, something in the way of an opposition, an opposition which, at first tentatively, then with an increasing certainty, looked towards the only living tradition capable of setting a great example: the Realist-Impressionist tradition which flourished in France. Whistler, a friend of Courbet and Degas, settled in London in 1859, and Legros, whom Baudelaire had praised, did likewise six years later, serving from 1876 until 1892 as head of the Slade School. Corot, Manet, Monet, Degas, Pissarro, Sisley and Lautrec all visited England, and the New English Art Club, founded in 1886, was established by painters who had studied in Paris. This growing opposition regarded as a threat a potentially influential national gallery in which pictures popular in subject as in treatment might set the tone. An article entitled 'The Sad Case of Mr Tate' expressed the view of the serious opposition at the prospect of a collection made up so largely of expensive purchases from Burlington House becoming the nucleus of a national gallery. 'Mr Tate,' wrote the anonymous critic–is it fanciful to identify him with Sickert?– 'Mr Tate . . . must certainly be credited with the contrivance of as costly a means of securing a back attic in the Temple of Fame as the ingenuity of man hath devised. That, whatever his ulterior motive, he has bought in good faith appears unquestionable; for "he proposes to invite a Committee of Experts"–R.A.'s to wit–"to sit in judgment" on his masterpieces, and chuck all such as "are thought by them" – that is, by this committee–"unworthy of a permanent place in a gallery of British Art." You can see, as through an atmosphere of crumbs and sherry–you can conceive the scene from here. The Committee of Experts–a Hanging Committee in disguise–making the round of a collection of things itself, in whole or in part, has placed upon the line in Burlington House; confirming its original estimate, or partial or collective, of a series of "works by Boughton, Fead, Peter Graham, Long, Alma Tadema, Gow, Stanhope Forbes (A.R.A.), Landseer. . . ." '[20]

Tate was indeed the friend of several Royal Academicians, particularly of Millais, who with Watts and Leighton was an ardent supporter of the projected gallery. He made his purchases, sometimes without discrimination, largely from Burlington House; he was, however, no partisan but a man who, although not articulate, was in fact increasingly possessed by a great vision: a representative gallery of the finest art of his native land, from the earliest times down to his own.

Two years, almost to the day, after the news of Tate's original offer to the Trustees of the National Gallery had been published, the writer[21] of a letter to *The Times* asked leave, in view of the 'unsurmountable difficulties' of finding a site for Mr Tait's [*sic*] picture gallery, to draw attention to a 'magnificent site' in Millbank, already in Government possession.

At the beginning of November well-founded rumours were in circulation that Sir William Harcourt, the Chancellor of the Exchequer in the new Government, had reopened negotiations with Tate, and that the selected site would be that upon which Millbank Prison stood. After two years during which nothing seemed certain but rancour, procrastination and disappointment, there was a change in the tide with regard to Tate's great project. A few misgivings were voiced about the site itself. 'It is altogether unsuitable, being full in the face of half-a-dozen manufactories, a pottery and a gas works. It is on the Thames, at a dirty spot. . . . Blue mould and green damp are the prevalent conditions of the region.'[22] *The Times*, extending a warm welcome to a project which it had consistently supported, described the site as 'one of the finest in London'.[23] It was, in fact, an interesting one. The space of three acres allocated for the new gallery formed only a small part of the extensive area, some twenty-four acres in all, upon which Millbank Prison stood, with its ten ranges of gaunt buildings, radiating like the spokes of a gigantic wheel, a building described by Jeremy Bentham as 'An English Bastille'. When the prison was built the site was little better than a swamp, famous formerly for its snipe, and taking its name from an old mill that had once belonged to the Abbots of Westminster. The demolition of the prison was put in hand before the end of 1892, and at the sale of the building materials there were offered, among other items, ten million bricks and more than two thousand iron and other doors.

The popularity of the new project was enhanced by the use of unemployed men on the demolition of the prison throughout the winter months.

The architect of Tate's choice, Sidney J. R. Smith, who had prepared plans for the galleries which Tate had hoped to erect in South Kensington and on the Blackfriars Embankment, now prepared further plans for the gallery at Millbank, and after successive modifications the final design was completed by the autumn of 1894, and an authoritative account, with plans and elevations, was published in *The Art Journal*. By February 1896 the building was sufficiently far advanced to be visited by a large party of members of the Architectural Association, and by the end of May 1897 it was virtually complete. 'Photographs of the building, in a forest of scaffolding', said Tate, 'were submitted to the late Sir John Millais, my deeply regretted friend, shortly before his death, and he endorsed in pencil the two words, "quite satisfied", beneath them.'[24]

EARLY YEARS 1897–1917

When it was opened the Tate Gallery consisted of the existing vesti-
bule, the seven galleries flanking the river, and the sculpture hall
demolished to make way for the much larger sculpture hall presented
by Lord Duveen and opened forty years later. The buildings covered
about an acre, and as the area allotted was three acres in extent there
was ample space for future expansion.

The large and miscellaneous collection assembled in the new building was made up as follows: the purchases made under the terms
of the Chantrey Bequest, transferred from South Kensington; eighteen
paintings by G. F. Watts recently presented to the new Gallery by
the artist; the Tate Collection consisting of sixty-seven pictures and
three bronzes (accepted in 1894), and ninety-six pictures by British
painters born after 1790, including a number from the Vernon collection, transferred from the National Gallery. In order to strengthen
the collection at the Tate a few works by Constable and Wilkie were
included, but, although the artist was born twelve years after the
deadline of 1790, it was decided to retain a number of Landseer's
pictures at the National Gallery – including *Dignity and Impudence.*
No works by Turner were included.

The new gallery was endowed, therefore, with a number of pictures of beauty and interest: *Ophelia,* by Millais, the finest of a group
of works by this artist included in Tate's gift, *Pegwell Bay,* by Dyce,
Derby Day, by Frith, and representative works by Bonington, Madox
Brown, Cecil Lawson, J. F. Lewis and Rossetti, besides those by
Constable, Wilkie and Watts already mentioned. Considering that
it was drawn from a heterogeneous group of collections and that no
attempt had been made in any one of them to form a representative
collection of British painting, it was inevitable that – in spite of
containing individual works of great distinction – it should lack

19

coherence, and be quite inadequate to represent the period in terms of its finest achievement. But however many deficiencies and defects the collection suffered, Tate's great project was at last realized. Not altogether, however, as he wished: the new gallery was not independent but subject to the control of the National Gallery; it was not a gallery of British art but only of modern British art. 'There probably never was', observed *The Sketch*, 'a public benefaction more criticized, scorned, and individually rejected than Mr Henry Tate's Gallery.'[25] It seemed, however, as though the entire nation were determined to make amends.

The Tate Gallery was opened, on 21st July 1897, by the Prince of Wales, afterwards King Edward VII; Tate was created a baronet and appointed a trustee of the National Gallery. The following lively and somewhat Proustian description of the opening ceremony was given by *The Daily Graphic*.[26]

'The larger number of the guests who went to the Tate Gallery on the site of Millbank yesterday to see it opened missed the symbolic part of the ceremony, which was the unlocking of the central door by the Prince of Wales, but it must by no means be thought that they missed the most interesting feature of the occasion, for this was undoubtedly the speeches. The Prince of Wales, with whom was the Princess of Wales, the Duke and Duchess of York, the Duke and Duchess of Fife, drove in semi-State from Buckingham Palace and were loudly cheered on their arrival at the new gallery....

'They went past the graceful pillared hall, with its plashing fountain and tall summer flowers ... to the room where the sixty-five pictures which Mr Tate has given are displayed. Here a gay throng of that portion of London Society which is seeing out the season to its bitter end was gathered, and welcomed the Royal party with a vigour undiminished by the warmth of a very crowded assemblage in a gallery where ventilators had apparently been hermetically sealed. The party of Royalties and trustees, benefactors and beneficiaries ranged themselves on a little platform at one end of the room immediately beneath the incongruous background of Lord Leighton's depressing *The sea shall give up its dead* – against which the bonnets of the ladies stood out with gay irrelevance. When the spectators had get down from their chairs and the cheering had ceased, Mr Tate came forward and delivered a dedicatory address to the Prince, candidly reading it from the roll of paper which he carried. It was a short speech, simply worded, and holding out a generous promise of additional buildings, should the necessity arise for them; and at its close Mr Tate, bowing, handed the deeds of gift of the gallery to the Prince. The Prince, with a word or two and a smile, took them and delivered them into the charge of the First Commissioner of Works, Mr Akers-Douglas: and from that moment the Gallery became irrevocably the property of the nation.' Sir William Harcourt, Leader of the Opposition, and Arthur Balfour, Leader of the House of Commons, both made speeches, and finally the Prince thanked Tate in the name of the British nation.

The Gallery was opened to the public on 16th August; its interest aroused by the extensive eulogies in the press, the public attended in great numbers.

The early history of the Tate Gallery was quiet, almost uneventful, in comparison with that of its conception. The first Keeper was Charles Holroyd, a capable etcher and a favourite pupil of Legros at the Slade, who retained his post until his appointment, in 1906, as Director of the National Gallery. The two principal events of his administration were the extension of the building and the establishment of a special collection of the work of Alfred Stevens. At the opening of the Gallery Tate promised, as already noted, to defray the cost of an extension, the plans for which were in fact, drawn at the same time as those of the completed building. Work on this was put in hand in December 1897 and the extension was opened on 28th November 1899; nine galleries were thereby added to the original eight making the Tate the largest art gallery London. The extension aroused widespread interest, and Queen Victoria herself 'left ... the Palace ... in an open landau drawn by four horses, with postilions and outriders. Seated in the carriage with Her Majesty were Princess Victoria of Schleswig-Holstein and a lady-in-waiting. Her Majesty's Highland attendants were in the rumble of the vehicle.'[27] The route was selected to enable Her Majesty to look at the Tate Gallery. 'When leaving the Palace Her Majesty was not wearing her spectacles, but on nearing the Tate Gallery at Millbank she put them on in order the better to see ... the handsome building.'[28]

In the year of its opening the Gallery became possessed of *Isaiah*, Stevens's full-size cartoon for his mosaic on a spandril under the dome of St Paul's. Shortly afterwards Holroyd circulated to the Trustees of the National Gallery a 'Statement or Apology' for his 'policy with regard to the works of Alfred Stevens', in which he referred to him as being, with Turner, the greatest artist of the nineteenth century, and to his own ambition 'to get together a room full' of his work, and he urged the acquisition of 'every fragment of his work we can get hold of'. It was not until 1910, after D. S. MacColl, the Tate's second Keeper, had brought to light the rejected Equestrian Statue of the Duke of Wellington, long hidden away in the crypt of St Paul's, and pursued his eloquent and learned advocacy of Stevens's claims to recognition, and an Alfred Stevens Memorial Committee had become active, that a unique special collection – which eventually included more than four hundred examples – of the work of that lofty and extraordinarily versatile genius came into being. The original idea, however, was Holroyd's.[29]

Early in the new century the honeymoon period was over, and criticism began to make itself heard. One cause of complaint was that the National Gallery sent modern foreign paintings, and mostly slight examples, down to the Tate. 'What have Horace Vernet and Ary Scheffer to do in a National Gallery of *British* Art?' enquired *The Graphic*. 'What right have Bonvin, Costa, Fantin-Latour, Salame, Clays, Rosa Bonheur, Charles Poussin ...?'[30] The National Gallery had not been extended, the pressure on its walls had grown continuously, and the temptation to transfer unwanted pictures, whether suitable or not, to the larger and less crowded institution under its tutelage was at times beyond resisting. A far more serious occasion for criticism was the administration of the Chantrey Bequest. The *Pall Mall Gazette* stated that of the £60,064 spent under its terms, £ 46,314 went to R.A.s and A.R.A.s, and only £ 13,750 to outsiders, and it concluded that 'some explanation is required from the President and Council of the Royal Academy as to their dealings with the funds left for the public benefit'.[31]

D. S. MacColl exerted a potent formative influence upon the character of the Tate. In its early years the Gallery was far from being independent: administratively it was subordinate to the National Gallery, whose able and scholarly Director, Sir E. J. Poynter, was elected in 1896 President of the Royal Academy. Moreover, the Tate was annually the recipient of the works of art bought by the Royal Academy through the Chantrey Bequest, in the choice of which the Keeper had, of course, no say whatever, and year by year it became more apparent that the general character of these works was entirely discordant with the emerging character of the Tate, with which the works of independent artists such as Stevens, Samuel Palmer, Madox Brown, Rossetti, Charles Keene, Whistler and Steer were in much closer harmony. The matter was critical, not only because it became increasingly irksome that an institution should have to accept unwelcome additions to its collection with regard to which it had no say, but because the income from the Chantrey Bequest was the only income regularly available for developing the Tate Collection. Indeed it remained virtually the Tate's only means of acquiring anything until after the end of the Second World War. It has, therefore, loomed large in the Tate's history, and its operation has constituted an anomaly which controversy, negotiation, minor administrative adjustments and much goodwill have never satisfactorily resolved.

It was some three years before he began to serve as Keeper of the Tate Gallery that MacColl began to take a hand in its affairs. Early in 1903 he had opened an attack on the administration of the Chantrey Bequest with the publication of two articles in *The Saturday Review*,[32] which in 1904 were reprinted with additional matter as a pamphlet. His criticism was factual and logical. It was also extremely forthright. It began by asking whether it was not clear that 'the provisions of the Will have been ignored, its intention perverted, and the funds . . .

23

grotesquely maladministered'; he asserted that the President and Council of the Royal Academy 'considered their duties accomplished when they had strolled round their own exhibition, and distributed this national trust as a prize-fund for the exhibition', and used it, moreover, 'to penalize those who do not exhibit'.

MacColl's charges were not new ones. A series of questions of hostile character had been asked in Parliament, and a demand for an enquiry, for instance, made by Sir Robert Peel as early as 1884.[33] What stirred public opinion was the startling contrast shown by MacColl to exist between the provisions of Chantrey's Trust and the manner in which it was administered. He published the relevant extract from Chantrey's Will – the text of which was then less accessible – in which the purpose of his Bequest is declared to be 'the purchase of works of fine art of the highest merit in painting and sculpture that can be obtained, either already executed, or which may hereafter be executed by artists of any nation, provided such artists shall have actually resided in Great Britain during the executing and completing of such works', and in which he required that the Royal Academy 'shall have regard solely to the intrinsic merit of the works in question, and not to permit any feeling of sympathy for an artist or his family ... to influence them'. Although no doubt against the sense of Chantrey's project it was, explained MacColl, technically permissible to purchase works 'executed in England by foreigners, in Roman, Mediaeval or Renaissance times'. In spite of the latitude allowed, the policy and practice of the Royal Academy had been – with insignificant exceptions – to make their purchases from their own current exhibitions, and by far the greater number from among the recent works of Academicians or of those who shortly became Academicians. At least twelve years had passed since any work had been purchased anywhere except from a Royal Academy exhibition; indeed there had been only two or three cases when pictures had been bought outside, and even then it was from a gallery that 'came to serve as an annexe to Burlington House'.

In considering the works in the Chantrey Collection MacColl does not discuss their absolute merit or demerit, but only their relative merit, i.e. whether they were, as Chantrey required, 'works ... of the highest merit ... that can be obtained'. He supposes the Chantrey Trustees in the witness-box, and obliged to answer the question 'Are or are not Stevens, Madox Brown, Holman Hunt, Burne-Jones-Fantin-Latour, Whistler ... [he might have added Monet, Pissarro] among the most eminent artists who worked in Great Britain from the time of Chantrey's Will till the present?'; and then obliged to answer whether the most eminent are, on the contrary, Joseph Clark, W. Hunt, W. Small, L. Rivers, A. Hacker, H. S. Hopwood, Mildred Butler, Lucy Kemp-Welch, A. Glendening, junr., J. Young Hunter and Charles Maundrell (to name only a few who figure in the Chantrey catalogue). It is inconceivable, he said, that they should answer 'no' to the first question and 'yes' to the second. 'Do they consider', he asked, 'that the English nation made a better bargain when they obtained a water-colour by Mr Cockram [whoever he may be] at £150, than the French when Mr Whistler let them have his mother's portrait for £160?' MacColl called for a Parliamentary enquiry. His charges were recapitulated in the correspondence columns of *The Times*, but no explanation was offered, and *The Times* commented coldly on the silence of the Chantrey Trustees, against whom *Truth* urged legal action.

The following year a Select Committee of the House of Lords, under the Chairmanship of Lord Crewe, was set up to enquire into the administration of the Chantrey Trust.

In the course of their extensive and wide-ranging enquiry the Committee examined a number of leading Royal Academicians upon the interpretation that they placed upon Chantrey's Will. Again and again such witnesses expressed the opinion that the testator's intention was primarily to confer pecuniary benefits upon living artists and their families, and subject only to the condition that the finest possible collection of paintings and sculpture should be formed.

THE EARL OF LYTTON: '... works of greater merit could have been bought if they had been able to buy them not from the artist direct?' [34]
SIR E. J. POYNTER, President of the Royal Academy: 'It is obvious.' [35]
LORD KILLANIN: 'I understand ... that you consider ... that the guid-

25

ing principle was that the money that was spent in this big bequest should go to painters; that the guiding principle was not, regardless of where the money went, that the most eminent works of Art of the day should be obtained?'

Sir L. A. Tadema, r.a.: 'Most decidedly.'[36]

Q.: 'There is nothing in his Will, is there, to support that view?'

A.: 'It is perhaps not worded in that way.'[37]

The Earl of Lytton: 'Supposing the Council refused to buy [a masterpiece] because the money ... would not ... go to an artist or his family ... would not that be doing precisely what the terms of the Will forbid, namely, considering the artist rather than the merit of the picture?'

Marcus Stone, r.a.: 'I agree that it suggests that [but] he refers to the artist as the person from whom the work is to be purchased.'[38]

Q.: 'But ... the only place where the artist and his family are referred to is in the clause in which he forbids you to consider them?'[39]

The Report concurred with the opinion of critical witnesses that the Chantrey Collection 'contains too many pictures of a purely popular character', and fails 'to give expression to much of the finest artistic feeling of its period', and that 'the unduly narrow construction placed on certain terms in the Will by successive Councils has had an unfortunate effect upon the collection'.

This early phase of the Chantrey controversy, and its culmination in the House of Lords Enquiry, served to foster the emerging, distinctive character of the Tate. The recommendations of the House of Lords Committee, largely ignored, did little to reform the operation of the Bequest, but the severe disapprobation expressed of the methods by which the Chantrey Collection was being made and of its quality served in a great measure to emancipate the new Gallery from Royal Academy influence. Two important witnesses, moreover, Roger Fry and Robert Dell, editor of *The Burlington Magazine*, advocated the creation of a completely independent Tate, separate from the National Gallery, to which the Chantrey's funds should be transferred.[40]

MacColl's appointment in 1906 as its Keeper seemed to set the seal of official approval upon the Tate's evolving an independent policy. This policy, however, he pursued with caution. Works by Holman Hunt, Rossetti, Sargent, Steer, Stevens, J. Havard Thomas and Wilkie, among others, were added to the collection, but the outstanding event of his Keepership was the opening of the Turner Wing for the accommodation of the Turner Bequest. Shortly before MacColl's appointment thirty-five paintings by Turner—twenty-one of them, including *Interior at Petworth* and *The Evening Star*, never before exhibited—were transferred from the National Gallery (where they had been rediscovered, in store, the previous year), repaired and placed in Gallery XVIII (the last of the rooms built by Tate to be opened to the public). On 6th May 1908 it was announced by Lewis (later Lord) Harcourt, First Commissioner of Works, that on the vacant site behind the Tate, an addition of five rooms on the main floor, with others below, would be made in the near future, through the generosity of J. J. (later Sir Joseph) Duveen, senior, and would be occupied by the bulk of the Turner pictures and drawings, transferred from Trafalgar Square. The Turner Wing (designed by Romaine-Walker, the donor's architect) was begun that August, and completed and arranged by the summer of 1910. Owing to the recent death of King Edward VII no formal opening took place, but King George V paid a private visit on 9th July and the public was admitted three days later. The original benefaction was considerably added to by Duveen's son, later Lord Duveen of Millbank, at whose expense a staircase was constructed to connect the five upper with the four lower rooms, and the whole scheme completed so as to house Turner's Bequest in a fashion more splendid than the artist himself could have hoped for.

In the meanwhile MacColl's health required him to accept a less arduous post, and in 1911 he was appointed Keeper of the Wallace Collection. Charles Aitken succeeded him as the third Keeper. He had been but a few months in office when a Committee was appointed whose findings were to be of crucial importance for the Tate.

For some years the increasing export of masterpieces had been the cause of widely shared concern. In 1903 a number of patriotic art lovers came together to form the National Art-Collections Fund, whose function it was to enrich the various public collections, more especially on occasions of threatened loss. The threatened export of the unique Velasquez, the 'Rokeby' *Venus* (eventually saved in 1905 by the benevolent exertions of the Fund), and the actual export of Rembrandt's *Mill*—one of fifty-three works by this artist to be lost to this country within a few years—thoroughly aroused public opinion.

In December 1911 a Committee of Trustees of the National Gallery, appointed by its Board to enquire into The Retention of Important Pictures in this Country and other matters connected with the National Art Collections, held its first meeting, under the Chairmanship of Lord Curzon. Their Report, published in 1915, conspicuous for its thoroughness, clarity and vigour, contained four recommendations which intimately affected the Tate. These were: the formation of a Gallery of Modern Foreign Art, to be erected on the vacant site behind the Tate; the gradual conversion of the Tate from a Gallery of Modern British Art (i.e. since 1790) into a Gallery of British Art; the partial administrative separation of the National and Tate Galleries; and the transfer of the administration of the Chantrey Trust to a Board of Tate Trustees. The formation of a Gallery of Modern Foreign Art, declared the Report, is 'not merely a duty imposed on us by the wise example of foreign countries, but is also essential to the artistic development of the nation', for which 'we in this country appear to possess neither policy nor method'.

The Report endorsed the aim of Sir Henry Tate that the Gallery he formed should be 'a National Gallery of British Art in all its branches', with the proviso that the great masterpieces should continue to be hung at the National Gallery, and recommended that the administration of the Tate should be placed under a separate Board upon which the Trustees of the National Gallery would depute members to represent them, and to these would be added a number of persons selected for their knowledge of, or interest in, modern art, and that the Keeper be advanced to the rank of Director.

But 'the dream in which we have indulged', declared the Committee, is not 'capable of realization until the Chantrey problem is ... solved', that is to say the presence in the Tate Gallery of a growing collection of works 'not because they have been selected, bought, or voluntarily accepted by the Trustees, but because they have been purchased by ... the Royal Academy under the terms of the Chantrey Bequest', which the Tate has 'been compelled to accept.... The administration of this trust, and its choice of works has been the subject of much public criticism, which culminated in the appointment of a Select Committee of the House of Lords', but its 'somewhat timid' suggestion that the purchases should be made by a committee of three specially selected persons had been disregarded. The opinion 'well nigh unanimously entertained by our witnesses the Report continued, was that the Chantrey pictures 'are a discredit to the walls of the gallery; the low standard set by them renders it impossible ... to invite distinguished British artists to sell their pictures at modest prices for the honour of being represented ... ; really valuable offers of pictures ... are withheld because of the distrust and hostility thereby aroused, and a number of the foremost British painters ... remain entirely unrepresented.' The Report favoured legislation releasing the income of the Chantrey Trust to the Tate. 'On the other hand,' wrote Lord Curzon, in a personal memorandum,[41] 'if such a procedure' [it had been suggested that matters be brought to a head by refusal to accept the Chantrey works] 'were thought to be too violent, the only alternative open to the Trustees would appear to be to act on the more limited ... powers which they admittedly enjoy, and, by a drastic exercise of the rights of storage ... to reduce the evil to less conspicuous dimensions.' Lord Curzon and his Committee manifested towards the Tate an ambitious solicitude. They were aware of its too narrow scope and of its many deficiencies, but the future they foresaw for it was a great one: 'A time will gradually come', they declared, 'when it will take its place as a worthy representation of British Art of all periods, and when London will be recognized as possessing two National Galleries of the first class, instead of one. In Trafalgar Square will always be visible the supreme glories of British painting, alongside of their fellows, but to Millbank the student will go who desires to follow the history and evolution of indigenous art.'

FIRST YEARS OF INDEPENDENCE
1917-1939

If half the world had not been at war when this admirable Report was published, its impact would doubtless have been more immediate, but even as things were it was not long before its principal recommendations began to be translated into facts. By a Treasury Letter and Minute of 24th March 1917 – the latter giving effect to the decisions of the Prime Minister, Lloyd George – the Tate Gallery was constituted as a general National Gallery of British Art without limit of time, but with special responsibilities for modern British art, and also as the National Gallery of Modern Foreign Art. The newly appointed Board of Trustees held its first meeting on 3rd April.

A national collection of modern foreign art had for some time been regarded as a matter of urgent importance. So long, however, as the nation was without the nucleus of such a collection the matter remained academic; but in the summer of 1913, given the possibility of the transfer to London from Dublin of Sir Hugh Lane's provisional gift of pictures as a consequence of the failure of his negotiations with the Dublin Corporation for the erection of a gallery of modern art, it became a practical issue. This provisional gift included the thirty-nine foreign paintings which eventually comprised the long-disputed Lane Bequest. These he offered as a loan to the London National Gallery, actuated in part by the hope that Dublin would accept his conditions; in part to gauge British sentiment about the desirability of a collection of modern foreign art for London. The loan was accepted on 12th August; on 8th September Dublin finally rejected Lane's conditions; and the following day, in an interview, Lane spoke of his hopes that the presence of his pictures might 'lead to the realization of [his] ambition [for] the establishment in London of a permanent Collection of modern international art'.

On 27th September he removed the thirty-nine pictures from the Dublin Municipal Gallery, then at Clonmell House; they reached Trafalgar Square some two months later. At this early stage, when the exhibition of his collection in London appeared imminent, Lane executed his Will, on 11th October, bequeathing them 'to found a collection of Modern Continental Art in London'. On 15th January 1914, however, the Trustees of the National Gallery informed Lane that, having viewed the collection, they would consent to the exhibition of only fifteen pictures, but that before doing so they wished to learn what his intentions were with regard to the future disposition of these fifteen. Lane replied indignantly on 12th February rejecting the Trustees' unexpected stipulation that a part only of his collection be shown. So far as a pledge about their future destination was concerned, he repeated what he had originally told Lord Curzon, the Trustees' representative, before the exhibition was agreed to in August 1913, namely that he would make no definite promise but that he would be greatly tempted to give the collection to London if he thought that the gift would mean that steps were taken to create a Gallery for Modern Continental Art, which he felt was 'a crying want'. The Trustees decided, however, that they could make no concessions to Lane's point of view and that the proposed exhibition at the National Gallery must be abandoned, and they informed Lane in this sense on 28th February 1914. The idea of an exhibition at the Tate Gallery – at that time also controlled by the National Gallery Trustees – was put to Lane by MacColl, one of his friends, and Lane replied that if MacColl and other friends (none of whom, however, were Trustees) were able to bring this about he would agree to it. For one reason or another the furtherance of this idea hung fire, although its proposers continued to hope that it would eventually be carried out, and in June Aitken obtained an assurance from Joseph Duveen the younger that he, for his part, would raise no objection to an exhibition of the collection in one of the Turner Galleries presented by his father. In May MacColl had discussed with Duveen the suggestion that he might consider the presentation of a new gallery for modern foreign art, Lane having confirmed that such a promise would decide him in favour of his pictures going to London, but nothing had so far come of this.

World War I broke out in August and shortly afterwards there ensued Lane's own death and the discovery of an unwitnessed codicil. On 3rd February 1915 Lane, who had been elected Director of the Dublin National Gallery almost a year before, executed a codicil to his Will in which he bequeathed the thirty-nine pictures to the City of Dublin on condition that a suitable building be provided for them within five years of his death. (A Parliamentary Committee of Enquiry formed in 1925 found by a majority of two to one that Lane was of the opinion that he was making a valid legal disposition.) This codicil was entirely in Lane's handwriting, was signed by him three times, but was unwitnessed. On 7th May, returning from a short stay in America, Lane was drowned in the wreck of the *Lusitania,* and the publication of his Will and of the unwitnessed codicil gave rise to a controversy the echoes of which are still reverberating. During the previous March and April he is recorded as having expressed his views about the future of his collection to a number of friends both in England and in Ireland. It is clear that he was anxious to feel assured of a worthy and secure home for it; but the interpretations put forward of his final intentions as between London and Dublin have been divergent. There was never any doubt, however, of the legal validity of the Will, and after Duveen learnt of this he decided that since Lane had thus provided a nucleus of a foreign collection he would himself offer to provide the gallery to house it. The offer was formally accepted in November 1916. In consequence the National Gallery of Modern Foreign Art was built as an addition to the Tate Gallery and opened by King George V, accompanied by Queen Mary, on 26th June 1926.

It makes a sad comment on human affairs that ever since the discovery in Lane's desk at the Irish National Gallery, shortly after his sudden death, of the unwitnessed and therefore invalid codicil to his Will, this Bequest has been the cause of bitter controversy. Irish opinion, deeply stirred and perhaps uniquely united, did not cease to urge Dublin's moral right to the thirty-nine pictures, and Dublin's case – which rests not only on the codicil but also on the testimony of persons of integrity, some of them very close to Lane and not all of them Irish – has attracted many ardent English supporters. Other people, whose integrity nobody questions either, who saw Lane shortly before he sailed for America, formed exactly contrary impressions of his intentions. Anyone who has researched into the history of the Bequest, in many places obscure, can hardly fail to be impressed by the moral cogency of the Irish case. But on the British side this recognition has been accompanied by the conviction that it was immoral and productive of endless public and private confusion to alter a legal disposition unless all the evidence points unequivocally to a palpable frustration of the testator's intentions. In this case there is weighty evidence that points in two opposite directions. It is melancholy that the generous and enlightened but enigmatic impulses of a man deeply ambitious of benefiting both the country of his birth and the country where he made his home – Ireland and England both moved him to love and to exasperation – should have been a cause, however unwitting, of protracted friction between them. Since 1959, however, the Lane controversy has been in abeyance, for in that year an agreement was reached between the Trustees of the National Gallery (to whom all the Lane pictures still at the Tate were transferred) and the Commissioners of Public Works in Ireland which provided for the division of the collection into two groups of approximately equal importance and their exhibition alternately in London and Dublin for periods of five years.

No sooner had the Lane pictures been placed on view in the Tate Gallery in 1917 than they began to exert their fructifying influence in a way which would have delighted their donor. There they were seen by a forty-one-year-old rayon manufacturer named Samuel Courtauld. A real 'eye-opener' is how he described the experience. '... I remember especially Renoir's *Parapluies*, Manet's *Musique aux Tuileries* and Degas' *Plage à Trouville*. ... I knew nothing yet of Cézanne.' Courtauld's enthusiasm for this master was not aroused until, some five years later, he visited an exhibition at the Burlington Fine Arts Club which included seven Cézannes.

There is a kind of collector who regards the works of art he owns as the most private among his private possessions, who is reluctant to show them lest they lose, as it were by exposure to all and sundry, something of their mysterious virtue. Courtauld's attitude was the very opposite: he was eager not only to show his pictures to his friends, but to share the aesthetic experiences which guided him to acquire them and the way in which these were heightened or diminished with the passage of time and closer intimacy. Presently such private communication ceased to satisfy him: he felt the need to share his enthusiasms more widely, and to meet the challenge of the public's indifference, or even hostility, towards the school of painting which he was convinced had a place apart. Only a few years, after all, had passed since the National Gallery had provoked Lane's indignation by declining to show more than a selection of the thirty-nine paintings he had lent. The impulses to share and to challenge found expression in a great act of vision and generosity, in the creation, in 1923, of a fund of £ 50,000 for the acquisition of modern French pictures for the Tate Gallery. This fund was administered by a committee of which the members were Lord Henry Bentinck, Sir Michael Sadler, Sir Charles Holmes, Director of the National Gallery, Aitken, and Courtauld himself. The Tate was thereby enabled to acquire, during the next few years, twenty-three paintings by Manet, Renoir, Monet, Degas, Sisley, Pissarro, Cézanne, Toulouse-Lautrec, van Gogh, Seurat, Utrillo and Bonnard. Of these superb acquisitions *Une Baignade, Asnières*, Seurat's first monumental composition, was the most breathtaking, but hardly less magnificent were Manet's *Servante de Bocks,* Cézanne's *Paysage Rocheux*, Renoir's *Première Sortie*, and van Gogh's *Tournesols* and *La Chaise et la Pipe*. In less than four years the Tate Gallery was enabled to take a place among the finest collections of modern French painting – a place which lack of funds and the transfer to the National Gallery of all the Lane and almost all the Courtauld pictures has made it impossible to maintain. Among the acquisitions from the Courtauld Fund were the first works to be acquired by any public collection in England of Bonnard, Cézanne, Seurat, Sisley, Utrillo and van Gogh. The prestige of the great collection of modern foreign painting established by Lane and Courtauld, and the fine new galleries in which it was hung, before long attracted further important accessions from other sources; such, for instance, as the Frank Stoop Bequest, in 1933, of seventeen foreign pictures that included works by van Gogh, the Douanier Rousseau, Matisse, Braque and Picasso.

A number of works by Sargent, presented or transferred to the Tate, were placed in a gallery provided for their display by Duveen, which was also opened in 1926 as part of the Gallery of Modern Foreign Art.

The Report of the Curzon Committee, the recommendations of which played a crucial role in transforming the Tate into a largely independent gallery of British painting of all periods, and called into being a modern foreign gallery as an addition to it, affected the intractable Chantrey problem only indirectly. The want of confidence in the administration of the Trust and the lack of respect for the purchases made under its terms shown by witnesses who gave evidence before the Curzon Committee warned those responsible of the dangers of continuing on the same path, and the newly constituted Board of the Tate at once showed its determination to explore the possibilities of reaching some solution through constructive co-operation with the Royal Academy, by signifying its readiness to meet representatives of the Council and Chantrey Trustees 'in friendly discussion'. Some half-dozen 'Chantrey Conferences' between representatives of these bodies were held, and although they led to no final solution a working agreement was arrived at. Its conditions were that no work should be purchased without notification to the Tate Board, which would take over nothing on which its opinion had not been ascertained; that the Board should be entitled to make proposals for the purchase of works by both deceased and living artists, and that the three bodies concerned should meet together from time to time. As a result of proposals made by its Board under this agreement the Tate was able so secure works which were invaluable additions to the collection, such, for example, as *Claudio and Isabella*, by Holman Hunt, a group of works by Burne-Jones (all in 1919), *Portrait of the Artist*, by Charles Keene, and *Hammersmith Bridge on Boat-Race Day*, by Walter Greaves (both in 1922).

The right granted to the Tate to bring proposals for purchases to the attention of the Academy was strengthened in 1922 by a new arrangement negotiated through the Treasury, whereby two Recommending Committees were set up, one for painting, the other for sculpture, consisting of two Tate and three Academy representatives, whose function it was to submit proposals to the President and Council. This arrangement gave full satisfaction to neither party; it resulted, nevertheless, in the purchase of a considerable number of particularly welcome acquisitions proposed by representatives of the Tate. These included *Mrs Raynes*, by Steer (in 1922), *A Waterfall*, by Innes, and thirteen cartoons and sixty drawings by Stevens (all in 1923).

The Tate's most important accession after its establishment as a collection of British art of all periods was a group of twenty illustrations in water-colour by Blake to Dante's *Divine Comedy*–his last, and in certain respects his most inspired, drawings. The unfinished series of one hundred and two drawings was sold by auction in 1918 in a single lot for £7,665 and purchased by a group of interested institutions and private collectors, formed on the initiative of the Tate; these drawings were afterwards divided up among the participants according to the amount of their contributions. The Tate at that time had no funds at its disposal, but grants were made on this occasion by the National Gallery, the National Art-Collections Fund, Lord Duveen and a number of other friends. From early in the Gallery's history there was a tacit determination to represent the work of this unique figure as fully as circumstances might allow: the acquisition of these celebrated drawings resulted in the establishment of a special Blake collection alongside those of Turner, Stevens and Watts. Some half-dozen examples the Gallery already possessed, and in 1923 the splendidly augmented collection was hung in a room specially prepared for it.[42]

Even from the summary account here given it will be apparent that the Tate's first decade as a largely independent institution was a prosperous time: the scope of the collection was extended so as to include all British and modern foreign painting; the collections themselves were improved in quality as they were increased in scale, and the administration was likewise expanded and consolidated. In the

New Year of 1928 its progress received a severe check. Early in the morning of 6th–7th January the Thames broke the Embankment walls and overflowed, and the lower floor of the Tate was flooded to a depth of over eight feet; considerable damage was done.

The nineteen thousand water-colours and drawings of the Turner Bequest were submerged. Some damage was done to a number of them, and a few, some of them small pencil studies, were lost.

Considering the time they spent immersed, however, in the turbulent and filthy water, they suffered, in the opinion of those best placed to judge, surprisingly little. In addition seventeen oil paintings, a plaster bust and two miniatures were severely damaged but repairable, and eighty-one oil paintings were slightly damaged.

The disaster had other consequences besides the material destruction it brought: it impaired the confidence of the public and the health of an invaluable servant. Together with other members of the staff and a few Trustees, Aitken salvaged works of art—at one time himself disappearing beneath the surface of the flood—and he never fully recovered from the strain to which this ordeal exposed him.

Just over two years later, on reaching the age of sixty-one, he retired. Aitken was a different kind of man from MacColl; MacColl was fervent and learned, incisive and elevated, one of the finest writers of his generation on the fine arts, and a most formidable advocate. In comparison Aitken was an ordinary man: his intelligence was relatively pedestrian, his powers of self-expression scarcely adequate; he seemed an unimpressive, retiring, dry person who, had he not been Director of the Tate, might have lived out his life without leaving any particular mark upon this world. But Director of the Tate he was, and the opportunities this position offered and the responsibilities it imposed brought out qualities that made him a great director: clarity and firmness of purpose, and a burning devotion to the Tate. He neither overawed, nor did he charm, but he impressed by his sincerity, his grasp of affairs, his rectitude, his modesty and a consistent fundamental good sense. His chief and instinctive admiration seemed to have been for the Old Masters, the Pre-Raphaelites and Stevens, for certain painters of his own generation, mostly associated with the New English Art Club, and he was far from insensitive to the qualities in the work of men of a younger generation; his admiration for the Impressionists was of later growth. His taste was dependable although neither original nor subtle, but, aware of its limitations, he constantly sought the advice of members of a small group of friends whose judgment he recognized as superior to his own. It was as a selfless co-ordinator of the gifts of others – one of the most precious gifts the director of a museum can possess – that Aitken was at his best. He was aware of his possession of this gift. In response to the tribute of admiration and gratitude paid him by the Trustees on his retirement, he declared that he was only entitled to credit in that he had recognized, registered and appreciated all the talent and goodwill which was lying latent at the service of the nation.[43]

Aitken was succeeded by J. B. Manson, himself a painter, who began his long period of service at the Gallery in 1912 as a clerk. It was unfortunate for Manson that he was not Director a few years earlier; his chief enthusiasm was for the Impressionists, but by 1930 these painters were splendidly represented by purchases from the Courtauld Fund, which was exhausted and could be revived only by the sale of pictures already acquired under its terms. Impressionist prices had risen and he had therefore little scope for this particular enthusiasm, and his interest in the work of the Impressionists' successors was not conspicuous.

The Contemporary Art Society had purchased in 1926, out of its newly created Modern Foreign Fund, *Têtes à Massacre ('La Mariée')* by Rouault, and *Liseuse à l'Ombrelle* by Matisse, specifically for presentation to the Tate. The Rouault, perhaps the finest work by this artist in Great Britain, was declined by the Gallery in 1932 and did not become part of the collection until 1935. The Matisse, after being declined twice, was only accepted in 1938. More puzzling still is the meagreness, during Manson's directorship, of the additions of works by leading contemporaries, even by painters with whom he himself was associated as secretary of the Camden Town Group: a single Spencer Gore, nothing by Gilman or Ginner; three Sickerts, however, were added, including the admirable *Aubrey Beardsley*. The Modern

Foreign Collection was enriched by the fine Stoop Bequest, already mentioned. The outstanding event of his directorship was the gift by Duveen of a huge sculpture hall with two annexes, which made the Tate the largest art gallery in the British Commonwealth, and which seems likely to remain, for some time at least, the last major addition to the building.

The lack of a gallery to house a national collection of modern sculpture had long been a matter of concern, and there had been discussions about such a project between the donor and the Board as far back as 1927. There already existed, at the Victoria and Albert Museum, a national collection of sculpture, which contained important examples of the work of many nations and periods, including a number of fine modern examples, but the presence of these last was almost fortuitous, as no attempt had been made to build up anything of the nature of a representative modern collection. The existing sculpture gallery at the Tate was too small and was intended only for the works of British sculptors.

The original project for the provision of a gallery for modern foreign sculpture was eventually broadened, and as a result the scope of the Tate was further extended: it was recognized as the National Collection of Modern Sculpture, both British and Foreign. The Sculpture Gallery, which is more than three hundred feet in length, thirty-six in width and fifty in height, was opened by King George VI, accompanied by Queen Elizabeth, on 29th June 1937.

At that time the situation with regard to modern sculpture resembled the situation with regard to modern painting when the Tate was first opened almost exactly forty years earlier. Although modern sculpture had been acquired by the Royal Academy through the Chantrey Bequest, and by the Tate Gallery itself as well as by the Victoria and Albert Museum, the accumulation by all three bodies had been entirely haphazard. When therefore Duveen's spacious hall was built, there was not much sculpture available of sufficient quality to withstand the scrutiny that such magnificent surroundings would attract or to deserve a place in a representative collection. There was the superb group of bronzes by Rodin, which the sculptor himself had presented to the nation and which was transferred from the Victoria and Albert Museum to the Tate, where, however, for some mysterious reason, most of them remained in store. In addition a few good pieces by Maillol, Stevens, Watts, Havard Thomas, Epstein, Dobson and a few others were already in the Gallery's possession. But before Manson had time to develop the new collection his health failed. Early in 1938, having served for twenty-six years as a member of the staff and eight as Director, he retired and the present Director was appointed to succeed him.

A beginning was shortly made with the introduction of the works of unrepresented artists of the contemporary generation. Two rooms hitherto occupied by Chantrey purchases, mostly of a popular Victorian character, were cleared and replaced first by late Turners hitherto unexhibited, and afterwards by the new acquisitions. These two became the last of a sequence of rooms in which the British Collection was arranged in as close accord with logic and chronology as the design of the building permitted, and the best of the works acquired under the terms of the Chantrey Bequest – a miscellaneous collection without organic unity – were integrated into the main collection, to which they formed a valued addition, and the remainder were placed in store. But over Europe 'the lights were going out', and the main preoccupation of the Gallery at that time was plans and preparations for the evacuation and safe keeping of the collection should a war break out.

THE WAR AND AFTER

The Second World War disrupted, of course, the normal life of the Tate, and 1939 marks a convenient point at which to review summarily the Gallery's history to that date. Forty-two years had passed since its foundation, and twenty-two since it had been accorded a substantial measure of responsibility for its own affairs, and during this time its progress had been extraordinary.

A fine collection of English painting had been brought together, which included unique special collections of Turner, Blake and Stevens and outstanding special collections of Watts and the Pre-Raphaelites. A good beginning had been made with the representation of the more illustrious among the senior living painters; Steer, for instance, by eighteen examples, Sickert by eleven, and John by eight.

The collection of later nineteenth-century foreign painting, thanks mainly to the generosity of Lane and Courtauld, was unmatched in Great Britain and by few similar collections abroad. This great achievement is the more remarkable if it is borne in mind that the Gallery was in receipt of no regular Government grant. Its only regular assets were small sums made available by the National Gallery and the funds of the Chantrey Bequest, over the expenditure of which its influence was slight and intermittent.

Owing to the wide extension of its scope, the Tate's obligations, however, were very great, and many things, therefore, remained to be accomplished. First and foremost the collections – both British and foreign – needed to be brought up to date: they contained no works by many of the leading artists of the contemporary generation, and others were meagrely represented. The representation of Constable was inadequate, and in comparison with that of Turner insignificant. There was a scarcely token representation of British painting before Hogarth.

Just before the outbreak of the war, the Tate's collections, in common with those of the other national galleries and museums, were removed to places of safety. Shortly after the beginning of the air attacks on London the Gallery itself suffered serious and extensive damage and by the end of the war every room had been rendered unfit for exhibition purposes.

The administration and the current records remained at the Tate until 1940, when damage by blast and floods made it necessary to remove the records to the country. They were brought back to London in 1943. An office was maintained at the Gallery throughout the war, but the staff was greatly depleted. After 1941 the administrative staff consisted only of the Director and one Assistant.

Owing to the removal, during the war, of most of the permanent collections of works of art, and to the rapid growth of interest in the visual arts, which was a characteristic manifestation of the enhanced seriousness of the national temper, there was an unprecedented demand for opportunities of seeing works of art, which there was, at first, no adequate means of satisfying. This demand—which did not abate with the conclusion of the war—led to the formation of the Arts Council and to a modification of policy with regard to temporary exhibitions. Temporary exhibitions had been held from time to time before the war, but the emergence of a larger and more exacting public called for far more frequent exhibitions, and with a rather different emphasis. Before the war, especially where modern art was concerned, these—one-man shows, of course, apart—were often assemblies of a more or less miscellaneous character. The new public demanded instruction as well as delight, and the exhibitions designed to provide this have accordingly a more closely integrated, in a word, a more didactic character. This new policy beyond doubt fosters the interest of the new public, but it cannot be pursued without some dislocation of the permanent collection.

During the war the Trustees and Director of the National Gallery came to the Tate's assistance and placed certain of their own rooms at the disposal of the Tate; the Gallery was able, therefore, to organize a series of exhibitions at Trafalgar Square. Between 1942 and

1946 there were held the Wilson Steer Memorial Exhibition, the first extensive exhibition in London of the works of Paul Klee, and two exhibitions of the Tate Gallery's acquisitions. Selections from the last two were subsequently shown in various provincial centres. In 1941, in conjunction with the National Gallery, the Tate held a large retrospective exhibition of the works of Sickert, and in 1946 accommodated an Arts Council exhibition of the work of James Ensor. In 1944 two exhibitions, 'British Narrative Pictures from the Tate Gallery' and 'Two Centuries of British Drawings from the Tate Gallery', were organized for provincial circulation.

At the end of the war, the damage to the Gallery having made it impossible to exhibit any pictures on its own walls, it was decided to make available to Great Britain's Continental friends and allies a selection of the best of its modern British pictures. Accordingly a representative collection of pictures of the last fifty years was selected by the Tate and shown by the British Council in 1946–7, in Brussels, Amsterdam, Copenhagen, Paris, Berne, Vienna, Prague, Warsaw and Rome. It is unlikely that any collection of modern British pictures had ever before attracted so many visitors on the Continent. On its return a selection was taken on tour by the Arts Council. The Gallery also organized for the British Council a representative exhibition of works by Turner, which was shown in 1947–8 at Amsterdam, Berne, Paris, Brussels, Venice and Rome.

At the end of the war, then, the Tate Gallery presented a melancholy spectacle. The huge building stood derelict, its glass roof entirely detroyed and replaced by tarpaulins which shut out all light from the galleries beneath – black dank caverns which smelt of burning and decay. Rubble and stone blocks were heaped against the exterior walls. Attendant staff were pitifully few in face of the vast and multifarious enterprise of packing up the pictures in their several places of refuge, transporting them to London, reframing them and hanging them up. In any case the sorely beset Ministry of Works – from which everybody was clamouring for something – was unable, for a time, to promise even walls to hang them on.

The enthusiasm with which exhibitions of serious painting were being received, and many other signs, proclaimed that the new public was rapidly expanding. It became the most urgent obligation to place the Tate building at the service of this new public with the briefest possible delay. But delay, inevitably, there was. At first no men, no materials, nothing was to be had at all. The two remaining members of the administrative staff, in overcoats and mufflers – rigorous winter lingered in the dark, windy, clammy interior of the Tate throughout the spring of 1944 – wandering from room to room, wondered how all this was to be accomplished or even begun.

Little by little, however, the stone corpse came to life; repairs, at first so modest as to be scarcely visible, were carried out. New staff, inadequate in number and no member of it with art gallery experience, were recruited and trained. And after the first desperate situation had been overcome it gradually became apparent that one of the war's consequences for art galleries in spite of, partly indeed because of, the destruction and disruption which it inflicted upon many of them, was to offer them opportunities without precedent for the adoption of policies more imaginative and more clearly defined and for radical reorganization.

The Tate's situation offered an opportunity, in short, exhilarating to contemplate, of a new start – an opportunity similar to that which opened out in 1917 before the newly created Tate Trustees. On 10th April 1946 the Gallery was reopened by Ernest Bevin, Secretary of State for Foreign Affairs, or rather, a tiny enclave of six galleries in a desert of dereliction. This enclave was at once put to intensive use. Before the end of the year it had accommodated six exhibitions, five organized by outside bodies and one by the Tate, including an important American exhibition, 'American Painting from the Eighteenth Century to the Present Day', which was the fruit of close collaboration between the Tate and the National Gallery of Art, Washington. The opening of this exhibition was attended by King George VI and Queen Elizabeth, and Parliament voted a contribution of £1,500 towards its cost.

From this time onwards a continuous series of exhibitions has been held. Some of them have been organized by the Gallery itself, others by outside bodies. Among the most successful have been the Arts Council's 'Van Gogh' (1947–8), 'Art Treasures from Vienna' (1949), 'Mexican Art' (1953), and 'Picasso' (1960). Those arranged by the Tate have been mainly retrospective exhibitions of the work of modern British painters, of which the series has included Matthew Smith, Stanley Spencer, Wadsworth, Wyndham Lewis and Francis Bacon.

It was not until three years later, on 24th February 1949, that Sir Stafford Cripps, Chancellor of the Exchequer, formally reopened the whole Gallery, and the final repairs were completed in the following year. Awareness of the opportunities offered by the war and determination to make good use of them were widespread, and one manifestation was the appointment in 1944 of a Committee by the Chancellor of the Exchequer and the President of the Board of Education 'to examine the functions of the National Gallery and the Tate Gallery, and, in respect of paintings, of the Victoria and Albert Museum, and to consider the working of the Chantrey Bequest'. The purpose of this Committee – of which the Chairman was Mr Vincent Massey – was to recommend a more logical co-ordination of functions between these three institutions, which had all grown up after a somewhat haphazard fashion.

Its principal recommendations were designed, so far as the Tate was concerned, to clarify and alleviate what it described as 'the incongruous position of the Tate Gallery and the restricted conditions under which, as the Gallery is at present constituted, the Board of Trustees and the Director must endeavour to serve its various and ill-defined objects'. These recommendations led to the formulation of the clauses included in the National Gallery and Tate Gallery Bill, for transferring the legal responsibilities for the Tate Collections – which had hitherto been vested in the Trustees of the National Gallery – to the Trustees of the Tate, while making provision for transfers between the two Galleries. This Bill was introduced in the House of Lords on 4th November 1953, under the title of The National Art Collections Bill; the second and third readings took place on 24th November 1953 and 3rd April 1954. With important amendments, including a change in its title, the Bill was introduced in the House of Commons on 4th April 1954, passed its second and third readings on 29th October and 10th November 1954, received Royal Assent on 25th November 1954 and came into force on 14th February 1955, thus, fifty-seven years and eight months after its opening, making the Tate fully independent. The Massey Committee, like its predecessors, the Crewe and Curzon Committees, recorded its opinion about the poor quality of the majority of the Chantrey purchases, and recommended that the administration of the income derived from the Bequest should, if possible, be transferred to the Trustees of the Tate. Legislation was not introduced for this purpose, but discussions between representatives of the Treasury, the Royal Academy, the Chantrey Trustees and the Tate led in 1949 to an agreement whereby the Tate was accorded three instead of two representatives on the two Selection Committees and the Royal Academy undertook not to purchase any work until it had ascertained that it would be acceptable to the Tate. No finality, however, has yet been reached; revisions of procedure still continue, with mutual cordiality and respect. Of the several compromises that have been framed to meet the intractable problem posed by the Chantrey Bequest none have answered to the full satisfaction of either party, but the Royal Academy has purchased at the suggestion of the Tate a number of works which the Gallery has signified that it regarded as particularly desirable acquisitions. There have entered the collection in this way since the beginning of the war such fine works as *The Artist's Mother* by Gertler, *The Artist's Mother* and *Interior* by Gilman, *W. B. Yeats* by Augustus John, *Nude, Fitzroy Street, No. 1,* by Matthew Smith, *The Resurrection, Port Glasgow* and *Joachim Among the Shepherds* by Stanley Spencer, *The Pool of London* by Derain, *Lytton Strachey* by Henry Lamb, *Brodzky* by Gaudier-Brzeska, and several bronzes by Epstein, to mention at random a few notably welcome Chantrey purchases.

High hopes are seldom completely realized, and lack of funds and of sufficient staff, chance and human frailty have prevented the complete realization of the hopes entertained for the Gallery at the con-

46

clusion of the war, but all of them have been realized in some degree.

In at least three respects the British collection is now more representative than it was before the war. Paintings have been acquired by Gower, Gheeraets, Isaac Fuller, John Michael Wright, Lely and other predecessors of Hogarth (who previously marked the Collection's point of departure) and since 1961 they have been shown in a gallery by themselves. In place of the scattered representation of Constable there has been assembled around *The Chain Pier, Brighton* – half the cost of which was voted by Parliament in 1950 – a collection of Constable's paintings, shown in a single gallery. This does not approach in scale the unrivalled collection of paintings by Turner in the adjoining rooms, but it is a worthy memorial to the greatness of a master who had been far from adequately represented. There has been built up, too, an outstanding collection of twentieth-century British paintings. It is now possible to show a sequence of works by British painters extending from George Gower, Serjeant Painter to Queen Elizabeth I, to young men still in their twenties.

The Blake collection, which had received no addition since 1922, has been rather more than doubled by the accession of no less than thirty-five works, thanks mainly to the generous enthusiasm of the late W. Graham Robertson, and it is now without a rival even in America.

In spite of these and other additions to earlier British painting, however, the greatest expansion has been in the representation of the twentieth century. At the outbreak of the war, the Gallery's most imperative need was that the collection of modern British paintings and sculpture should be brought up to date. Henry Moore, Frances Hodgkins, Ben Nicholson, L. S. Lowry and David Jones, for instance, were unrepresented; and hardly more justice was done to such artists as Wyndham Lewis, Paul Nash, Mark Gertler and Matthew Smith. During the war years, while contact with the Continent was reserved, the obvious and most rewarding policy was to concentrate on modern British painting. Then or in the following years these deficiencies were, therefore, made good; in addition works by Pasmore, Coldstream, Piper, Bacon, Sutherland, Ceri Richards, Burra, Le Bas, Moynihan, de Maistre, Herman, Medley, Nolan and Scott as well as numerous works by members of succeeding generations, were acquired; while the representation of their seniors such as Steer, Sickert, Ethel Walker, Augustus and Gwen John, Grant, Gilman, Ginner, Gore and Stanley Spencer was substantially strengthened.

During the war, too, from the Montague Shearman Bequest of 1940, important pictures by Matisse, Rouault and Utrillo were added and the Hindley Smith Bequest of the same year added six other modern foreign pictures. Among other important acquisitions were fine examples of the work of Chagall, Ernst, Kandinsky, Klee, Kokoschka and Modigliani. But peace made possible a more systematic attempt to fill, so far as resources allowed, some of the collection's gaps, to take account, in some measure, of recent developments in France and elsewhere.

Some beginning, then, was made with filling conspicuous lacunae. At the same time this measure of progress encouraged the devising of a more systematic purchasing policy. A policy of enlightened opportunism was no longer enough. By systematic policy is meant not simply, of course, a not haphazard policy, but a policy deliberately contrived to secure that all significant moments of a major artist's work or of an important movement should be adequately represented. But the purchase of an example of the work of a particular artist, of a particular subject or at a particular point in his development, is apt to be considerably more costly than the purchase of any worthy example of the work of any worthy artist. Even though the total funds available to the Trustees have increased, the building up of the collections has become, for this reason, a more costly undertaking; and the continuous and spectacular rise in the price of works of art has made very acute the financial disability under which the Trustees have to discharge their responsibilities towards the three collections under their care. Any detailed treatment of this disability would be outside the scope of this introduction. It is sufficient to observe that the total aid from the Government for the purchase of works of art available to the Gallery during the last forty-five years, that is to say since 1917 – the year when it was given its own Board of Trustees –

48

until the end of 1961 has totalled only £ 175,450, a sum which today would not represent much more than a tenth of the price of Seurat's *Une Baignade*. The Gallery, however, has not wanted for generous private benefactors and for aid from those invaluable friends of public art collections, the National Art-Collections Fund and the Contemporary Art Society.

It has never been possible, however, with these resources adequately to implement a systematic policy in regard to modern foreign painting. But since the end of the last war a number of important foreign acquisitions have been made, including *Notre Dame*, of 1900, by Matisse, a Friesz of 1904, and a splendid Fauve Derain, *The Pool of London*, of 1906. Three works of the highest quality, Picasso's *Buste de Femme* of 1909, his *Femme nue Assise*, painted a little later, and Braque's *Still-life with Fish* of 1909–11, provided the Gallery with its first examples of Analytical Cubism. Representation of the later phases of Cubism was strengthened by the addition of two works by Gris and two by Marcoussis. Among other acquisitions were three Légers and a later Rouault. Six Chagalls added to the collection included *The Green Donkey* of 1911, the first gouache made after his arrival in Paris, and two sketches presented by the artist himself, studies for decorations at the Watergate Theatre, London. The Gallery also acquired its first paintings by Giacometti, Miró and Masson and its first oil by Dufy.

The priority which the School of Paris must be accorded has made it difficult to represent other developments as fully as is desirable. Among Italian pictures acquired since the war are, however, a large de Chirico, two Sironis (one a collage from his Futurist period), two water-colours and a large oil by Guttuso and a characteristic still-life by Morandi. The Gallery is still very weak, however, in German twentieth-century art; three pictures by Klee have been purchased, making four in all, and three paintings by the *Brücke* artist Karl Schmidt-Rottluff have been presented. Works by the American painters John Marin, Maurice Sterne, Mark Tobey, Morris Graves, Bernard Perlin, Jackson Pollock, Rothko, Guston and Brooks have also been added to the collection.

49

As a result of these developments it may be said that the foundations have been laid of a collection of modern foreign paintings appropriate to the requirements of a great capital city. But compared with the collections available elsewhere it is still very inadequate, and must necessarily remain so while the funds at the disposal of the Trustees are so limited. Visitors to the Gallery who rightly admire the wealth of first-class works of the Impressionist school at present hanging on its walls will note what a disquietingly high proportion of these are loans liable at any time to be withdrawn. There is no room for complacency about the number of modern masterpieces owned by the nation either here or at the National Gallery.

In 1950 and again in 1961 a number of the most important French paintings of the nineteenth century in the collection were transferred to the National Gallery. Transfers of this kind fulfil one of the Tate's most essential functions, for it is a prime justification of such a gallery that as recent achievements recede into the past there should be found among them works which merit a place in the collection of established masterpieces. This process is likely to be a continuous one, and visitors who from time to time miss a work which has become familiar at Millbank may feel compensated by the opportunity to watch history in the making.

The traffic is not, of course, one way. It was intended by the National Gallery and Tate Gallery Act that the relations between the now wholly independent Tate and the National Gallery should be as close and harmonious as they had been in the past, and this, in fact, is what they are; each Gallery cedes works to the other in accordance with the respective functions of both.

But it is the enlargement of the collection of modern sculpture that has been, perhaps, the most notable development at the Gallery in recent years. When Lord Duveen's spacious new sculpture gallery was opened in 1937, apart from the collection of Rodin bronzes the Tate possessed little sculpture of note: since then the collection has been virtually transformed. The representation of the great French painter-sculptors is now good. Four more bronzes by Degas have been acquired, including *La Petite Danseuse* of 1880–1, the only sculpture by him that was exhibited during his lifetime. Renoir's two most important bronzes, *La Laveuse* and *Venus Victrix*, have been purchased, as well as bronzes by Picasso and Matisse (including his great series of four reliefs, *Nu de Dos*). Further important works by Rodin and Maillol, *Le Baiser* and *Les Trois Nymphes*, a bronze by Despiau, several more portrait busts by Epstein and Gill's carving *Mankind* have been added. The purchase of a bronze by Stevens and the gift of two marble portrait busts of English sitters by Carpeaux have strengthened the earlier part of the collection, and more recent work is represented by Moore (by whom the Gallery now possesses no less than twenty carvings and bronzes), Brancusi, Lipchitz, Laurens, Manzù, Arp, Butler, Hepworth, Giacometti, Pevsner, Gabo, Marini, Frink, Paolozzi, Chadwick, Armitage, Meadows and Wotruba.

In the sixty-eight years that have passed since the acceptance of Tate's gift to the as yet unbuilt gallery the Tate Collection has grown from the sixty-seven paintings and three sculptures to a collection of nearly four thousand British paintings, over three hundred modern foreign paintings and over three hundred and sixty pieces of modern sculpture, and, in spite of the proud obligation to transfer its finest acquisitions periodically to the National Gallery, both the quality and the representative character of the collection have been continuously improved. In the face of the acute and continuous limitation of finance and staffing under which the Gallery's three national collections have been built up, each in its sphere is without an equal among the art collections of the British Commonwealth.

The Tate Gallery of today does indeed wear a different look from what it did in its early days. Inevitably so, and the reason lies not only in the natural circumstances of its evolution and growth; the multiplicity of its aims contributes perhaps most of all. Reference has already been made to the various functions that the Gallery has come to exercise; for instance, that its permanent collection should house British painting, past and present, modern foreign painting, and modern British and foreign sculpture. To attempt to fulfil these various aims has, of course, some drawbacks, and a tidier segregation of functions has its appeal. But the advantages preponderate.

A mixed gallery is a corrective to any idea of the Old Masters as men who have never lived like other men but who have always shone like some eternally remote and subsistent luminaries in a world of timeless Platonic essences; it enforces the truth – which must be understood if art is to be even remotely comprehended – that artistic creation is not divisible into old and new but is a continuous process, always changing yet always the same, the outcome of man's struggle to create images to express his response – whether it be amusement or wonder, fear, curiosity or delight – to the world in which he finds himself.

Indeed a gallery only of established masterpieces, skimmed off, as it were, from the art of their time would be like a city whose every building was an architectural triumph that has alone been allowed to survive from among its fellows. With what relief would a visitor to such a city leave it to wander along country byways and to enjoy the variety offered by a cottage and manor house, village church and barn. If a man is familiar only with selected masterpieces of British poetry and prose, he is not very likely to understand intimately what poetry and prose writing are, or for the matter of that to appreciate what makes a masterpiece a masterpiece.

An understanding, and a relish for any period, and of the classics of any period, would seem to demand at least an aquaintance with the period's ebb and flow, with the 'feel' of the period, and accordingly with those works of it whose distinction is secondary and which fall short of being classics. Moreover, 'it is by no means clear', Professor Auden wrote recently, 'that the poetry which influenced Shakespeare's development most fruitfully was the greatest poetry with which he was acquainted. Even for readers, when one thinks of the attention that a great poem demands, there is something frivolous about the notion of spending every day with one. Masterpieces should be kept for High Holidays of the Spirit.'[44]

THE PLATES

BRITISH SCHOOL

WILLIAM DOBSON 1610–46
Endymion Porter c. 1643–5
Canvas 59×50 (150×127)

This portrait is the best known, and among the best, of a smallish group of paintings, mostly portraits, and less than sixty in number, the work of the finest English-born painter 'in large' before Hogarth.

Little is known about the painter. All that survives of his work appears to have been done at Oxford during the Civil War, between October 1642, when the Court and the headquarters of the royal army were established there, and June 1646 when the city was surrendered to the Parliamentarians.

Of Dobson's life at Oxford, where he painted portraits of members of the royal family and of the officers of the king's army, there is almost no record. No doubt the disorders and uncertainties of a society at war fanned his known inclination to riotous and extravagant living. After the surrender of Oxford he returned to his native city, London, where he was imprisoned for debt, and he died in extreme poverty at the age of thirty-five.

It was formerly the custom to associate Dobson with van Dyck, but there is no evidence of personal contact between them, and their pictures are as sharply distinct in method as they are in the view of life which informs them. Van Dyck's suavely handled canvases, elongated and silvery – toned, perfectly reflect and exquisitely enhance the precarious, romantic elegance of the Court before the War. Those of Dobson, squarish, roughly textured, glowing stormily, reflect, not less faithfully because obliquely, the tragedy that has come upon the country. With extraordinary insight he manages to catch the despair that haunts his often swaggering, ruddy-faced soldier-courtiers.

SIR PETER LELY 1618–80
Two Ladies of the Lake Family c. 1660
Canvas 50×71¼ (127×181)

Lely was a resourceful draughtsman, fertile in invention, at times a lovely colourist, and a man of incessant industry: his conspicuous talents made him the dominant portrait painter in England during the middle years of the seventeenth century. No portrait painter of comparable distinction was ever so little interested in the human face, and the vastness of his practice, and its predominantly courtly character tended to extinguish the small flame of his curiosity. Occasionally it blazed up, less rarely stirred by the features of men than of women; the best of the *Flagmen*, or Admirals, at Greenwich include several of the most conspicuous examples. But something about the two unknown ladies who are the subjects of this portrait – considerable research has failed to discover precisely who they are – compelled Lely to see them as engrossing personalities. He put them in a conventional setting skilfully adapted to show them off. The tired-faced, large-featured elder lady, placed against drapery, is the perfect foil to the younger, whose piquante, slightly exotic beauty has for a background a vista of woodland. The elder lady is a little marred by the parallel positions of her fluttering hands – common defects of Lely's figures – which draws attention to them; but upon the younger he has lavished all his extraordinary skill: her posture, the folds of her dress, the musical instrument which her hands caress, combine in a languid harmony which charms the senses.

The fact that the two ladies are manifestly real people lends a moving credibility to a picture which, were it otherwise, would be mere evocation of a Restoration Arcadia.

WILLIAM HOGARTH 1697–1764
The Graham Children 1742
Canvas 63^1/$_4$×71^1/$_4$ (160.5×181)

The subjects of this picture are the four children of Daniel Graham, Apothecary to Chelsea Hospital. The family is thought to have come to know the artist through his close friend Dr Benjamin Hoadley, Bishop of Winchester, whose portrait by Hogarth also hangs in the Tate Gallery near *The Graham Children.*

The scene has appropriately been likened to a miniature stage upon which the curtain has gone up to reveal the four children engaged in a performance not for an audience but for one another: the brother plays the bird-organ to the goldfinch, at which the cat—surely one of the best portraits of a cat ever made by an English painter—is gazing intently; the elder sister looks after the baby and the younger dances.

Hogarth was at his happiest in painting not official commissions but informal portraits of his friends. The conversation piece, the informal group portrait, offered special scope for his dramatic sense, his robust or tender sense of humour, his fascinated understanding of human beings in their relationships with one another. The pull of dramatic or psychological interest at times distorted Hogarth's arrangement of his figures and their accessories, but in *The Graham Children* there is no sign of such distraction: here, both formally and psychologically, the four children, the cat and the bird are knit together in a harmony which reflects the happiness that Hogarth felt in the company of his friends, and it is one of the finest paintings of its kind.

WILLIAM HOGARTH 1697–1764
O *The Roast Beef of Old England! ('Calais Gate')* 1748
Canvas 31×37¹/₄ (78.5×94.5)

For many painters the subjects they choose to represent are no more than
pretexts for the expression of their delight in certain forms and colours or
in the contemplation of certain persons, objects or places. There are other
painters for whom their subject is something more important than this.
Some painters, in brief, wish to communicate an aesthetic experience; others
wish to communicate experiences of other kinds as well. To this latter class
Hogarth decidedly belonged. He declared his wish 'to compose pictures on
canvas similar to representations on the stage', and his hope was that they
would be judged by the same criterion, and that they would be 'of the
greatest public utility'. In the art of Hogarth the ideals and the prejudices
of the artist, both as individual and as citizen, are forcibly expressed.

O *The Roast Beef of Old England!* is not among the very greatest of
his paintings, but its subject offered a perfect pretext for the expression of
certain of his most fiercely cherished ideas – ideas which were fanned to
white heat by the circumstances which the picture represents. Hogarth
detested the French for the tyrannical character of their government (which
he was for ever contrasting with the freedom conferred by British institutions) and for what he believed to be their laziness, their affectations, and
the 'superstitions' inseparable from their religion. In 1748 he undertook a
journey into France – the last and probably the first occasion when he left
his native land. At Calais, on his way home, he was prompted to make
a sketch of the ancient and so-called English Gate, which bore, he said,
'some appearance of the arms of England on the front', dating from the
time when the place was in English possession. As he drew he was arrested
and brought before the Governor as a spy. According to the account he
gave of the affair Hogarth was obliged to prove himself an artist by making
sketches, which included the landing of 'an immense piece of beef for the
Lion d'Argent, the English inn, and several hungry friars following it'. The
episode inspired the subject of this note.

The artist himself can be seen sketching; the hand and pike behind him
presage his imminent arrest. One of the picture's most engaging qualities is
the contrast between the harshness, even the brutality, of the satire and the
opalescent delicacy of the colour.

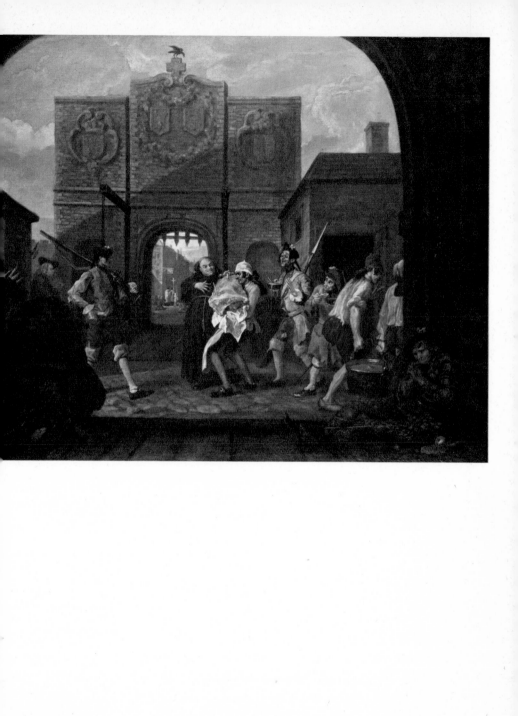

JOSEPH WRIGHT, OF DERBY 1734–97
An Experiment on a Bird in the Air-pump 1768
Canvas 72×96 (183×244)

During his life Wright took a high place in the regard of some of the most eminent men of his time (Josiah Wedgwood wrote of his shining gloriously in his profession), yet outside his native Derby he has suffered, since his death, an extraordinary degree of neglect. The obscurity that has for so long hung about his name shows signs of lifting, and with good cause, for Wright was a painter of rare originality and high gifts. In the subject of the present note and *The Orrery* at Derby he was the first painter to express the scientific enthusiasms of the age. He was in fact on intimate terms with a number of the scientists, industrialists and inventors without whom there would have been no Industrial Revolution. The attitude towards science manifest in his work was at once highly romantic and humanistic. Wright was an artist who delighted in contrasts: between the inexorable processes of science and the curiosity and awe which they inspired in mankind (especially in children); between the works of nature and the works of man, expressed sometimes by the contrast between the cold light of the moon and the fiery glare of the furnace, or the comfortable glow of the lamp, and between sheer light and sheer dark.

All this can be clearly read in the picture illustrated here. The method of painting which he adapted to serve these various and impressive ends was that of the powerful realistic art of Caravaggio – an art in which emphatic chiaroscuro played a principal part – which came to him by way of Honthorst, Schalken and other of Caravaggio's northern followers.

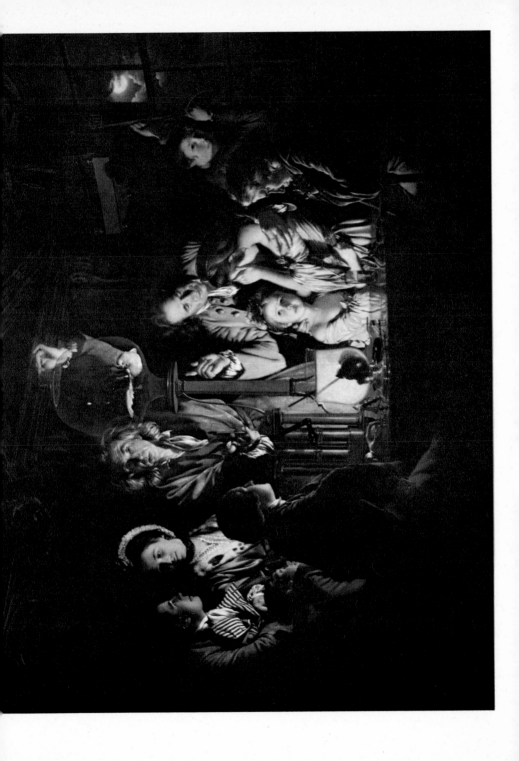

RICHARD WILSON 1714–82
On Hounslow Heath c. 1770
Canvas 17³/₄ × 21³/₄ (45 × 55)

'With Richard Wilson', wrote Ruskin, 'the history of sincere landscape art founded on a meditative love of nature begins in England.' It must be a matter for regret that the Tate Gallery does not possess a first-class example of the work of the painter who did for English landscape what Reynolds did for English portraiture; who found it provincial and made it a part of the European tradition – a tradition in which under his successors, Turner and Constable, England played a brilliantly original part. Although its point of departure was the modest tradition of English topography, the art of Wilson was formed during the six or seven years he spent in Italy, where he was deeply and permanently captivated by the magic of the ancient world and where he learnt from Claude and Gaspard Poussin the means of recreating Arcadia. Back in England he continued to paint Italian landscapes from studies made during his years in Italy, but it is mainly on account of his English, and more conspicuously still his Welsh, landscapes that he justifies the claim made on his behalf by Ruskin. In the best of these he represented the face of his native land in terms of the great classical tradition, but with a radiant elevated poetry and an intimate feeling for nature, especially her golden or silvery light, that was his own. The Thames Valley – the subject of the picture reproduced here, of which there are at least three other versions – was, after the Snowdon region of North Wales, the part of Britain in which he most delighted.

SIR JOSHUA REYNOLDS 1723–92
The 4th Duke of Marlborough and his Family c. 1776
Canvas 21⅝×19⅞ (55×50.5)

No one has ever less resembled the notion of the typical artist entertained by the public or represented in the pages of fiction than Sir Joshua Reynolds: he was cool, businesslike, an intellectual and accomplished man of letters. He was a man who had not only an ideal for his own art, but for the art of his country: he wished it to be no longer provincial but to become European. To this ideal his writings, which include some of the most rational and the most constructive criticism of his own or any other age, his conduct of the affairs of the Royal Academy, and to a large extent his own practice as a painter, were all dedicated. The impulse to observe closely and to represent faithfully what he observed was strong in Reynolds, but he subordinated this innate tendency towards realism ('nature . . . is not to be too closely copied', he warned his students) in order to master the grand style, deriving from Michelangelo, Raphael and Annibale Carracci.

The picture here reproduced is a sketch for the picture painted in 1777, which represents his most uncompromising and his most exuberant exercise in the grand style – so uncompromising and so exuberant that the spectator, seeing it for the first time, might well wonder whether it is the work of an English painter at all. The finished picture, which is at Blenheim, differs in several respects from the sketch, and is the most monumental not only of Reynolds's portrait groups but in all British portraiture.

The Duke was a man of cultivated interests: he presented five copies of cartoons by Raphael (as well as a large telescope) to Oxford University, of which he was made a Doctor of Civil Law in 1763.

Reynolds spent the whole of August 1777 at Blenheim making portraits of members of the Duke's family. The story is told that when he was working on the final version of this picture, he used to drop his snuff, and the Duchess, anxious for her carpet, sent a footman to sweep it up, to whom the painter said, 'Go away. The dust will do more harm to my picture than my snuff to the carpet.'

SIR JOSHUA REYNOLDS 1723–92
Lady Bamfylde 1776–7
Canvas 93³/₄×58¹/₄ (238×148)

In the eighteenth century the making of a portrait conceived as a simple
record of a sitter's appearance was despised as a menial task. Reynolds
accordingly evolved, between about 1760 and 1780, a grand classical manner
of making portraits, of which the painting here reproduced is a characteristic
but not an outstanding example. Reynold's portraits of this kind are so
familiar that they are often assumed to represent a widely prevalent style:
in fact this style – a curious blend of elements taken from the old masters,
in particular the Bolognese, with the characteristics of the subject, suffused
by a highly personal conception of 'sublimity' – was the invention of Reynolds himself. He continued to make portraits in this extreme classical style
until 1782, when, after a journey to Flanders and Holland, undertaken the
previous years, his sense of character reasserted itself and his colour became
richer, probably under the influence of Rubens.

THOMAS GAINSBOROUGH 1727–88
The Market Cart 1786
Canvas 72^1/$_2$×60^1/$_4$ (184×153)

The picture here reproduced – one of the most famous of all Gainsborough's landscapes – belongs, like *Musidora*, to the last phase of his art when he was engaged upon the creation of an Arcadia that would be wholly credible. His Arcadia was compounded of two elements: observation and poetry. Compared with that of his predecessors the landscapes of Gainsborough were so fresh, so closely observed, that he seemed to some of the most perceptive men of his own and later times to be a realist. 'If Gainsborough did not look at nature with a poet's eye,' said Reynolds in his moving discourse upon his great rival, 'it must be acknowledged that he saw her with the eye of a painter; and gave a faithful, if not a poetical, representation of what he had before him.' 'I fancy I see Gainsborough', wrote Constable, 'in every hedge and hollow tree', and Gainsborough himself has told us that there was 'no stem or post in or around my native town that I did not treasure in my memory from my earliest years'. Yet it would be an error to think of him, especially in his later years, as 'a natural painter' in the sense in which Constable called himself 'a natural painter', a painter, that is to say, of portraits of particular localities, at particular times of day, who regards his art as a science which 'should be pursued as an enquiry into the laws of nature'. There is in the landscapes of Gainsborough a reticence about the particular, a pervasive air of generalization, that surely tells us that we are looking not at the actual but at an ideal world. The pictures are sufficient evidence of this idealization, but we have Gainsborough's word in confirmation of it. To Lord Hardwicke, a patron who evidently asked him to make a painting of some particular place, he wrote, 'Mr Gainsborough ... shall always think it an honour to be employed in anything for his Lordship, but with respect to real views from nature in this country he has never seen any place that affords a subject equal to the poorest imitations of Gaspar or Claude. ... Mr. G. hopes that Lord Hardwicke will not mistake his meaning, but if his Lordship wishes to have anything tolerable of the name of Gainsborough, the subject altogether, as well as figures, etc., must be of his own brain! otherwise Lord Hardwicke will only pay for encouraging a man out of his way ...'

JAMES WARD 1769–1859
Regent's Park: Cattle Piece 1807
Canvas 28³/₄×46 (73×117)

The painter of the picture here reproduced was one of the strangest figures in the whole history of British art. Outstanding gifts, industry and lofty conceptions combined with a vanity that verged upon madness, with self-pity, cantankerousness and a total want of judgment, to form a personality made for tragedy. Born in a London slum, son of a 'settled sot' of a fruit-salesman, put to work at five – the early life of James Ward might have been written by Dickens. He received neither education nor training as a painter, but by his own efforts he acquired impressive technical resources. During his middle years he won a great reputation as a painter of animals and land-scape, but a commission to paint an allegorical triumph of the Duke of Wellington stimulated him to a grandiose attempt to proclaim himself the supreme history painter, the supreme poet of the ages, to crush rivals, to overwhelm spectators.

Inevitable and ludicrous failure brought down his reputation in ruins, and the last thirty years of his long life he spent in rancorous retirement.

The absurdity of his pretensions, manifest in a vast output of inferior works, and the conspicuous and unrelieved ugliness of his conduct have ob-scured the extraordinary power of his best paintings. A sight, in 1804, of Rubens's great landscape *The Château de Steen,* in the studio of Benjamin West, who had it for restoration, struck a deeply responsive chord in Ward's imagination and stirred him to fruitful emulation. The largeness of feeling, the energy, the richness and masculinity latent in Ward were released by the impact of this masterpiece. All these qualities, and a knotty, muscular power and a sense of drama peculiarly Ward's own, are present in the picture here reproduced, in the Tate's sombrely impressive *Goredale Scar –* too big for reproduction – and in a whole series of splendid pictures of animals and landscape. When Géricault visited London he particularly admired the paintings of Ward. Had Ward's powers been directed by some-thing of the intellect of Géricault or Delacroix he might have been a leader in the Romantic movement in painting.

WILLIAM BLAKE 1757–1827
God Creating Adam 1795
Colour print, finished in water-colour; the only known version 17 × 20⁷/₈
(43 × 53)

During his lifetime William Blake was unknown to all but a handful of
his countrymen, and those who knew him or his work mostly thought him
mad – even men of such understanding as Wordsworth, Lamb and Southey.
For nearly forty years after his burial in a pauper's grave he was forgotten.
The publication of his *Life* by Gilchrist, in 1863, brought a widespread
interest in his work and personality, and in about half a century he had
come to be ranked among the most illustrious of Englishmen, and the most
original of English artists.

In so far as it is possible to distinguish between the form of a work of
art and the spirit that informs it, it is true to say that the form of Blake's
art is compounded of various elements taken from the art of others – most
conspicuously the recumbent Gothic effigies in Westminster Abbey and prints
after Michelangelo – but the spirit is of an originality rarely equalled. 'I
must create a system', he wrote, 'or be enslaved by another Man's', and he
evolved an entire system of thought and a mythology to which both his
painting and his poetry are related.

The picture here reproduced is by general consent among his most powerful creations. The fact that his idol Michelangelo in the sublimest of his
paintings had treated of the same intractable and awe-inspiring subject did
not deter Blake. The Jehovah in the Sistine Chapel, sweeping across the
heavens, creates without effort and with a single gesture the Adam who is
the reincarnation of Apollo. Before a huge sun sinking in a twilight of blue
and purple, Blake's Elohim, spent by the Act of Creation, his great wings
scarcely able to bear him up, hovers over prostrate helpless Adam, already
in the toils of the Serpent who shall bring about his Fall. In technical
mastery Blake was in comparison with Michelangelo an ill-educated child,
yet the exalted intensity of his imagination has here enabled him to create
a hardly less memorable image of God's work on the Sixth Day.

WILLIAM BLAKE 1757—1827
Beatrice addressing Dante from the Car c. 1824–7
Water-colour $14^{5}/_{8} \times 20^{5}/_{8}$ (37×52.5)

'Men think they can copy nature...' Blake declared; 'they will find this
impossible, and all the copies ... of nature ... prove that nature becomes to
its victims nothing but blots and blurs.' Blake's sayings in support of the
exclusion from art of visual experience are today often quoted with approval
by those whose purposes they suit, but in fact this exclusion at times opposed
insuperable obstacles to the exact and unequivocal expression of Blake's
own vision. He denied himself the natural imagery with which to embody
his ideas, and lacking this he fell back, again and again, upon his recollec-
tions of works of art, or even, perhaps, consulted his folio of prints (scholars
have traced many of his numerous borrowings to their sometimes surprisingly
remote sources). But just as a student who has learnt to draw from nature
may be able eventually to represent nature accurately from memory, so
Blake won the power of creating, without recourse to other works of art,
a language perfectly adapted to communicate the ideas and images which
formed in his mind or else were evoked by the written word; for almost
all his paintings and drawings are illustrations, especially of the Bible, or
of the works of Milton, Dante or William Blake. This personal and precisely
expressive language became in his later years an instrument of extraordinary
power – a power never more manifest than in his last great undertaking, the
series of illustrations to Dante's *Divine Comedy*, left unfinished at his death.
In these wonderful works he seems to have entered into an intimate though
by no means uncritical communion with the spirit of Dante, and to have
added something of his own to Dante's divine message. Blake was one of
the greatest of illustrators yet never a subservient one: in the picture here
illustrated he creates an immediately recognizable illustration of the triumphal car described in the *Purgatorio*, but he also infuses it with a vast
complex of symbolism drawn from the highly unorthodox system of ideas
of his own creation.

THOMAS GIRTIN 1775–1802
The White House 1800
Water-colour 11³/₄×20³/₈ (30×52)

Girtin began as an accomplished topographer, but in the last years of his brief working life he attained the power of comprehending a wider horizontal sweep of landscape in a single emotional mood that conveys its grandeur. In order to draw the eye towards the distant prospect of plain, hillside, city or river, he was apt to leave his foregrounds featureless. Of

this power *The White House*, perhaps his most famous work, is a moving revelation. This drawing is, as it were, a window opening upon a serene prospect, wide and remote, of both banks of the Thames. In the gathering dusk gleams the white house itself, casting its white reflection far along the still surface of the river. The rays of the setting sun behind them deprive neither house nor reflection of a scintilla of their haunting whiteness, but the fact that this does not strike the spectator as incongruous is testimony to the serene power of Girtin's imagination.

SIR THOMAS LAWRENCE 1769–1830
Princess Lieven c. 1820
Canvas 18¹/₄ × 15¹/₄ (46.5 × 39)

'Weakened and harassed as Lawrence was by the habits of society', wrote Benjamin Robert Haydon, 'there were always gleams of power about him that made me lament that Nature did not quite finish his capacity.' An extraordinary brilliance in the handling of paint, the power, in the words of the poet Campbell, of making one 'seem to have got into a drawing-room in the mansions of the blest, and to be looking at oneself in the mirror', made him illustrious throughout the civilized world to a degree attained by no other English painter. It would be an error, as Haydon's admirable judgment implies, to consider him as he was for a time considered, and not rather as a graceful and dexterous but superficial, even slightly flashy, painter. His soaring sense of romance often dwindled into senti-mentality; his painting could be so suave as to vitiate the illusion of hu-manity in his subjects: there is much indeed that may justly be urged in criticism of Lawrence. Delacroix complained, for instance, of his exag-gerations and false effects, citing his portrait of Benjamin West, in which the head is brilliantly lit but the rest has no share in the light whatsoever. But at inspired moments the latent power of which Haydon wrote did not gleam; it blazed. The assembly of splendid portraits in the Waterloo Room at Windsor constitutes an achievement beyond the powers of all but very few painters of the nineteenth century. The Tate, though it possesses a number of Lawrence's portraits, has none to compare with these. *Princess Lieven* is beautifully sure and clear in form, and, small, uncompleted frag-ment that it is, it has something of that aura of grace and distinction that Lawrence was so often able to evoke.

JOHN CONSTABLE 1776–1837
Dedham Water-Mill c. 1819
Canvas 21×30¼ (53.5×77)

Constable was one of those who receive their deepest and most enduring impressions at the beginning of their lives. In what is perhaps the most illuminating of his letters he wrote '. . . the sound of water, escaping from milldams, over willows, old rotten planks, slimy posts, and brickwork – I love such things. . . . I . . . paint my own places best; painting with me is but another name for feeling, and I associate "my careless boyhood" with all that lies on the banks of the Stour. These scenes made me a painter, and I am grateful; that is, I had often thought of pictures of them before I had ever touched a pencil.' So intense were these impressions that they continued to incite his faculties to function at their highest pitch, and it is in scenes along his native valley that he showed his deepest insight into the character of places, and of the skies above them; where he most often captured 'the freshness and sparkle – *with repose*', at which he aimed. Even Brighton he disliked, a place, he wrote, where 'the magnificence of the sea, and its . . . everlasting voice, is drowned in the din and lost in the tumult of stage-coaches – gigs – "flys" etc.,' and where there was nothing for a painter 'but the breakers – and sky – which have been very lovely indeed and always varying'.

The picture here reproduced is either a full-size sketch for the finished picture at the Victoria and Albert Museum, or else the beginning of a final version abandoned when the artist decided to introduce a boat on the extreme left. The warm comprehension with which the subject is envisaged and the existence of several versions of it suggest that it was a favourite theme.

JOHN CONSTABLE 1776–1837
Chain Pier, Brighton 1824–7
Canvas 50×72³/₄ (127×185)

The quality for which of late years Constable has been most revered is the brilliancy of his response to nature: to rivers and trees and clouds and sea. This reverence is far from ill-founded. He came nearer than any painter had ever come to representing, in his own often quoted words, 'light – dews – breezes – bloom and freshness; not one of which has yet been perfected on the canvas of any painter in the world'. It was his communication of such natural effects in sparkling colours and with free, energetic brush strokes that so deeply impressed Delacroix and several generations of French landscape painters. But brilliant response to his sensations before nature did not constitute the whole of his art. For a painter to be content to do no more than this is to restrict the scale of his pictures, to give them the character of sketches and to hamper the effective expression of ideas. We know both from his letters and from the fact that he painted large pictures that he aimed beyond the representation of nature. 'I did not think', he wrote after a visit to a popular landscape painter, 'his things were quite so bad. They pretend to nothing but an imitation of nature ...' Constable painted a number of big pictures, and the progressive versions by means of which he evolved them testify to the importance he attached to them. Constable called himself 'a natural painter', by which he meant a painter of normal vision, yet he was a lifelong student of the old masters and his mind was filled with their compositions, which exerted upon his own a gentle, elevating discipline. There is a dignity and an expressiveness about his big pictures which give them qualities that no sketch can possess. The picture reproduced here, for all its splendid evocation of vast space, hurrying clouds, agitated waste of water and the 'wet light' which was his own discovery, does not quite rank with the greatest of his paintings.

It was probably painted at Hampstead in the winter of 1826–7. Much of the sparkle, however, must have gone out of it, for a year after it was painted a friend wrote to him, 'I wish, if *Brighton* is not out of your possession, you would put it on your easel again and mellow its ferocious beauties.'

SAMUEL PALMER 1805–81
A Hilly Scene c. 1826
Water-colour, pen and tempera, heavily varnished, on panel
$8^1/_5 \times 5^2/_5$ (21 × 13.5)

A believer in the mystery of God, a mind illuminated and uplifted by the reading of the great English poets, a youth upon whom Blake had conferred his friendship and had taken walking in the fields, Samuel Palmer had a vision of the land of Beulah, of a divine serenity and fertility, which guided him to make in his early years a series of landscapes of breathtaking beauty. He was able to perceive 'the soul of beauty through the forms of matter': his works, that is to say, are the product of an eye that was almost as precisely observant as it was visionary. The vision is the more memorable for being expressed in terms so familiar to our own experience. When he was nineteen years old he wrote in a sketch-book – and the words might serve as a description of any of his early pictures – 'So exquisite is the glistering of the stars through loop holes in the thick woven canopy of ancient elm trees – of stars differing in glory, and one of prime lustre piercing the gloom – and all dancing with instant change as the leaves play in the wind that I cannot help thinking that Milton intended his "Shady roof, Of branching elm *star Proof*" as a double stroke – as he tells of the impervious leafy gloom, glancing at its beautiful opposite – "Loop holes cut through thickest shade" and in them socketed the gems which sparkle on the Ethiopic forehead of the night.'

   The subject of this note belongs to the inspired group of early Kentish landscapes made during Palmer's 'visionary years' – his twenties and early thirties – and around the Kentish village of Shoreham.

J. M. W. TURNER 1775–1851
The Shipwreck: Fishing Boats endeavouring to rescue the Crew c. 1805
Canvas 67½×95 (171.5×241)

When he made this picture Turner was thirty, by which time he had given himself an education of extraordinary completeness. He was an industrious student; he early formed the habit of storing both memory and notebook with a vast mass of impressions and facts; he learnt all that he required from his masters and his rivals not so much by studying, or even by copying, their works, as by challenging them on their own ground by making original paintings in a style close to theirs. One of the painters whom he thus emulated was the Dutch sea-painter Willem van de Velde, the younger. (*Calais Pier*, identical in size and similar in style to *The Shipwreck*, was painted two or three years earlier.) 'That made me a painter', Turner once exclaimed in front of one of his paintings, and he did indeed paint a number of sea-pieces with his example evidently in mind. But the difference between the waves in *The Shipwreck* or *Calais Pier*, the difference between waves that so marvellously capture the intricate rhythms of the ocean's surge and its overwhelming power, and the ingenious conventional waves upon which the Dutchman's warships ride, provides a classic illustration of the difference between genius and talent. 'To wreathe a sculpture out of the waste wrath and torment of the sea', according to one discerning critic, 'was his supreme triumph.' Such was not the view of influential members of the Royal Academy when *The Shipwreck* was first shown. Difficulties within this institution in the early years of the century appear to have decided Turner to build his own gallery in which to hold exhibitions of his own works, and it was completed in 1804. The following year he included *The Shipwreck* in such an exhibition. Farington recorded in his *Diary* that the President of the Royal Academy, West, described the pictures which Turner showed there as 'tending to imbecility', and that to another Academician they appeared 'rank, crude and disordered'.

J. M. W. TURNER 1775–1851
House beside River, with Trees and Sheep c. 1807
Canvas 38×45 (96.5×114)

The attempt made by Turner through his engravings to reach a public beyond the influential artists and men of taste among whom he found little understanding gave his reputation a somewhat popular character. It was perhaps this circumstance that persuaded the men of taste of a later day to accord him a treatment so grudging–one of them, Roger Fry, went so far as to express doubt 'whether Turner ever did have any distinctive personal experience before nature'. Turner's achievement has also been somewhat smothered by the sublime but profuse and not always well directed praise of Ruskin, and his output–greater than any other British painter's–has made the study of his work an intractable undertaking. From these or other causes, and in spite of the growing disposition to revere Turner as perhaps the one master of the British School who has earned a place in the company of the great masters of European painting, there remains, nevertheless, an extraordinary disparity between the fabulous power and range of his achievement and the degree of attention paid to it by scholars.

There exists, for instance, a group of paintings to which *House beside River, with Trees and Sheep* belongs. These have not been the subject of particular study, yet they are of the greatest beauty and interest. They range from completed paintings to studies, and they all appear to represent scenes along the rivers Thames–between Walton and Windsor–and Wey, and to have been made about 1807. To judge from the stretches of river in their foregrounds, most of them would seem to have been painted from a boat; there is evidence which suggests that Turner had the use of a boat on the Thames. It is possible that they were among the first, perhaps the first, oil paintings to be completed on the site. They were made a number of years before the small studies from nature which are justly regarded as among the chief glories among the works of Constable. In the Thames and Wey paintings (which were considered unworthy of exhibition for half a century after they came into national possession) Turner combines an understanding of landscape unprecedented in British painting with an extra-ordinary degree of tenderness and grace.

J. M. W. TURNER 1775–1851
Rocky Bay with Classic Figures c. 1828
Canvas 35¹/₂×48¹/₂ (90×123)

No one except Turner could have painted the picture here reproduced. Its sentiment derives in part from Claude, whom Turner revered, but in one respect it differs radically from an analogous subject by Claude. The Arcadia of Claude, for all his mastery of the effects of sun and mist, for all his assiduous study of nature, was a frankly artificial creation. As Goethe expressed it, his 'pictures have the highest truth but no trace of reality. Claude Lorrain knew the real world by heart, down to the smallest detail, and he used it as a means to express the world of his noble soul. . . .' This world is one in which the beholder is not invited to a literal belief: it is an invented magical world of classical and Arcadian landscape. The facts of history and archaeology are disregarded: the very arrangement of his compositions in distinctly defined succeeding planes parallel with the picture's surface suggests not real landscape but the scenery of the theatre. It is scarcely too much to say that all this is but a pretext for the weaving of a lyrical spell that lingers still in the European imagination.

Turner was no less of a poet than Claude, but he was a painter of greater resource who lived in an age that science was beginning to transform. In the evocation of poetic moods he had to appeal to the greater knowledge of nature and sophistication of his own age and to use to their fullest his own wider powers. For Turner to express himself in Claudian terms would have been almost to affect simplicity.

Unlike a painting by Claude this painting, although it is suffused by sentiment that has much in common with Claude's, is wholly convincing. The measure of Turner's powers is the fact that he has been able to persuade us that even such an extravagantly beautiful scene as *Rocky Bay with Classic Figures* actually exists, that it could be photographed and surveyed.

J. M. W. TURNER 1775–1851
Petworth Park: Tillington Church in the distance c. 1830
Canvas 25×55 (63.5×139)

It was in 1802 with the purchase of a sea-piece that the third Earl of
Egremont began his great collection of Turner's paintings (which are still
at Petworth and were exhibited at the Tate in 1951), and in 1809 he commissioned Turner to make a painting of Petworth, his house in Sussex. This
was perhaps the occasion of his first visit, but it was probably not until
about 1829 that he became a constant visitor to the house.

At Petworth, the genius of Turner blossomed with an unprecedented brilliance. He made paintings of the park and the surrounding country (the painting here reproduced is one of the studies for the finished paintings still at Petworth), and some hundred water-colours on grey-blue paper, swift dazzling notes of action and character. At Petworth the last of the inhibitions that the busy world imposed on Turner were resolved, and he was free to see the world as light and movement. Genius is so commonly frustrated by apathy or persecution that Turner's sojourn at Petworth must ever be valued as one of the most fruitful episodes in the history of English painting.

J. M. W. TURNER 1775–1851
Venice: the Piazzetta from the Water c. 1835
Canvas 36×48 (91.5×122)

Turner first visited Venice in 1819, where, according to his habit, he made a number of sketches; but his first Venetian oil paintings were not exhibited until 1833. He made two subsequent and equally brief visits to Venice, in 1835 and 1840. It is strange that his first oil paintings of the city appear to have been made fourteen years after he first left it. Various explanations, none of them conclusive, have been put forward for the sudden stirring of long-dormant memories. For whatever reason, he continued to exhibit Venetian painting until 1848. He also painted purely for his own satisfaction a number of Venetian subjects which he never exhibited, and which were in his studio at the time of his death and formed part of the Turner Bequest to the nation. These were at first withheld from exhibition as of insufficient importance, and many of them were so encrusted with dirt as to be invisible.

The picture here reproduced was placed on exhibition for the first time, after cleaning, as recently as 1955. The group of paintings to which it belongs, which does not consist only of Venetian subjects, is one of Turner's most original achievements. Their subjects are mere pretexts for the creation of self-sufficient poems in colour and light, visions of an opalescent delicacy yet evocative of the vastness of the universe. It is not known when this picture was painted; the brown patches over the Doge's Palace have no apparent connection with it, yet without them the picture would lose in balance and cohesion.

J. M. W. TURNER 1775–1851
Yacht approaching the Coast c. 1840–5
Canvas 40¹/₂×56 (103×142)

Neither his early conformity nor his long celebrity afforded the later work of Turner protection from the most vulgar abuse. A certain clergyman, in an attack upon modern painters in 1836, described Turner's *Juliet and her Nurse* as 'thrown higgledy-piggledy together, streaked blue and pink, and thrown into a flour tub. Poor Juliet has been steeped in treacle to make her look sweet ...' The criticism is remembered only because it provoked Ruskin, then seventeen, 'to the height of black anger' and to writing in Turner's defence. *The Athenaeum* described three of his paintings shown in 1841 as 'wonderful fruits of a diseased eye and reckless hand', and one of them, according to *The Times*, represented 'nothing in nature beyond eggs and spinach'.

These being the terms in which journals of standing referred to the exhibited work of Turner, they would have been at a loss for words had their critics seen the paintings in which he expressed himself without reserve. These, however, he withheld from public exhibition, well knowing the reception they would be likely to receive. It is in his unexhibited oil sketches that the culmination is reached of Turner's attempt to create an art of pure colour. A number of writers have hailed these chromatic symphonies as anticipations of the paintings of the Impressionists, but to regard them in such a light is to misunderstand them. The aim of the Impressionists was to take by surprise, as it were, a fleeting moment of life, and to represent it, just as it was, frankly subject to all the limitations imposed by continually changing light, and, for preference, light at its brightest. The Impressionists were realists of a particular kind. Turner was not. Many of his late colour symphonies closely resemble their subjects, for Turner was a wonderfully precise recorder of all the phenomena of nature. But such resemblance was incidental to a different aim: he was a poet, and his eventual aim was to make poetry in terms of colour. In this poetry nature is not lost; it is transformed. The picture here reproduced is an example of this kind of poetry.

WILLIAM HOLMAN HUNT 1827–1910
Claudio and Isabella 1850
Oil on panel 30¹/₂×18 (77.5×45)

In his autobiography Holman Hunt protested at length against the claim of Ruskin and many others that Rossetti was the prime mover in the Pre-Raphaelite movement, and he advanced the counter-claim, with the support of much evidence, that the primacy belonged instead to Millais and himself. Rossetti was in all the operations of his mind a poet, and a nonconformist even to the principles laid down by his friends and companions of the Brotherhood. Hunt, on the contrary, was a puritan with a broad vein of pedantry in his composition, a man who rejoiced – if he ever rejoiced – in the inflexible application of inflexible principles – application so tenacious, so little reflective, that neither his skill nor his integrity, nor his heroic capacity for taking pains, could redeem it from absurdity. However good the case he argues, it may be suspected from the circumstances that his finest pictures were painted while he was on terms of intimacy with Rossetti, that the contact with a mind so imaginative, so capable of searching thought, yet so humorously zestful, was not devoid of benefits. Among Hunt's finest pictures – though it ranks below his masterpiece *The Hireling Shepherd* – is *Claudio and Isabella,* which is greatly to be valued for the exhilarating cool clarity of its form, its jewel-like colour and a candour that disarms. Nothing could less resemble, for instance, the hot, aggressive pedantry that marks every staring inch of his *Shadow of Death* painted some twenty years later.

The picture here reproduced owes its existence to the benevolence of a fellow painter, Augustus Egg (represented in the Tate by *Past and Present,* a Victorian tragedy in three episodes), who, after an older painter had first asked Hunt to submit designs for a picture he intended to commission, and then denied this intention and insulted him, himself commissioned *Claudio and Isabella.*

SIR JOHN EVERETT MILLAIS 1829–96
Christ in the House of His Parents 1850
Canvas 33½×54 (85×137)

Millais was one of the strangest enigmas that the history of modern painting offers to the contemplation of the student: a man of transcendent talents,
who painted pictures when scarcely more than a boy which are masterpieces not only of execution but also of intense poetic insight, who throughout his life showed intermittent gleams of power, yet who sank throughout
the greater part of it as a painter into an almost pathological triviality of
vision and execution. The key to the enigma may be that he lacked a hard
core of personality and accepted his ideas from those who mattered to him
most, whether the austere poetic ardour of the companions of his youth or
the vulgar standards of the plutocracy in whose ranks he eventually took
his place. It must be a matter for thankfulness that this suggestible genius
fell as a young man under the hypnotic spell of the ardent idealism and the
luminous intelligence of the young Rossetti. The picture here reproduced
was painted when the Pre-Raphaelite Brotherhood's brief existence was at
its most intense, and when Millais was only twenty-one years old. This
remarkable picture gave particular offence for being a too literal representation of a sacred subject, for representing the Holy Family as real
people instead of a pious myth, for treating them, in the words of *The
Athenaeum,* 'with a circumstantial Art language from which we recoil with
loathing and disgust'. The most virulent criticism came from Dickens: 'In
the foreground of that carpenter's shop is a hideous, blubbering red-haired
boy in a nightgown who appears to have received a poke in the hand from
the stick of another boy with whom he has been playing in an adjacent
gutter, to be holding it up for the contemplation of a kneeling woman, so
horrible in her ugliness that ... she would stand out from the rest of the
company as a monster in the vilest cabaret in France, or the lowest gin-shop
in England.'

FORD MADOX BROWN 1821–93
Carrying Corn 1854
Oil on panel $7^1/_2 \times 10^1/_2$ (19 × 27)

Recent criticism has begun to place the Pre-Raphaelites in a wider context
than had been the case hitherto and to see the style which they so suddenly
evolved not as an isolated English manifestation – whether mere eccentricity
or flash of genius – but as part of a European movement aiming at clarity
and exactness and with mediaeval preoccupations perceptible, for instance,
in the work of the German Romantics and in that of Ingres. Little has yet
been done, however, to assess the extent to which the Pre-Raphaelites shared
the realist impulse which moved Courbet and the Impressionists to transform
the painting of the Western World. This is no place to develop so important
and so intricate a theme; it is sufficient for the occasion to enquire by whom,
on the Continent of Europe, was made in the year 1854 so uncompromising
an essay in the art of representing landscape under full sunlight, with the
violet-coloured shadows, generally accepted as an Impressionist discovery,
as the picture reproduced here? Not by Courbet or the painters of Barbizon;
of the oldest Impressionists Degas was still a law student and Pissarro had
not arrived in Paris, while the First Impressionist Exhibition was twenty
years ahead.

There is an entry in the artist's diary for 4th September 1854 which tells
us of the beginning of this little landscape: 'About three out to a field, to
begin the outline of a small landscape. Found it of surpassing loveliness.
Cornshocks in long perspective form, hayricks, and steeple seen between
them – foreground of turnips – blue sky and afternoon sun. By the time I had
drawn in the outline they had carted half my wheat: by today all I had
drawn in was gone.' Another entry, made on 21st July of the following
year, gives an indication of his attitude towards landscape, and, incidentally,
of his awareness of colour in shadow: 'How despairing it is to view the
loveliness of nature towards sunset, and know the impossibility of imitating
it! – at least in a satisfactory manner, as one could do, would it only remain
so long enough. Then one feels the want of a life's study, such as Turner
devoted to landscape; and even then what a botch is any attempt to render
it! What wonderful effects I have seen this evening in the hayfields! The
warmth of the uncut grass, the greeny greyness of the unmade hay in furrows
or tufts with lovely violet shadows, and long shades of the trees thrown
athwart all, and melting away one tint into another imperceptibly; and one
moment more a cloud passes and all the magic is gone.'

DANTE GABRIEL ROSSETTI 1828–82
The Wedding of St George and Princess Sabra c. 1857
Water-colour 13¹/₂×13¹/₂ (34×34)

Though their movement triumphed, the Pre-Raphaelites abandoned the strictness of their original practice, with the tenacious exception of Holman Hunt. The aim was the representation of an imagined scene, not conventionally, not vaguely, but in full light, sharply and minutely, just as it might have actually been enacted, and not by accepted 'types' but by individual men and women. The effort and the stamina called for by the practice of an art of so intense a kind were phenomenal. Millais, the ablest of the Brotherhood, a painter and draughtsman of a technical ability in his lifetime unexcelled, commenting on the Brotherhood in later life, observed that 'one could not live long doing that'. The water-colour here reproduced is one of a group of five made for William Morris by the movement's most original and most intensely imaginative member and all now belonging to the Tate.

A passage in a letter from James Smetham, a poetic but fragile painter, well describes the picture and illustrates the way in which Rossetti's early work affected his contemporaries: 'One of the grandest things,' it runs, 'like a golden, dim dream. Love "credulous all gold", gold armour, a sense of secret enclosure in "palace-chambers far apart"; but quaint chambers in quaint palaces, where angels creep in through sliding panel doors, and stand behind rows of flowers, drumming on golden bells, with wings crimson and green. There was also a queer remnant of a dragon's head which he had brought up in a box. . . .'

WILLIAM DYCE 1806–64
Pegwell Bay, Kent–a Recollection of 5th October 1858 c. 1859–60
Canvas 24³/₄×35 (63×89)

Fortunate is the painter whose technical resources are commensurate with
what he has to communicate. Those at the command of the Douanier
Rousseau were just sufficient to enable him to share his marvellous epic
vision of innocence. Haydon's ideas were vivid and lofty, but the insuffi-
ciency of his means brought him frustrations and death. Dyce was Haydon's
tragic opposite: he was accomplished, disciplined and well-schooled in the
Florentine tradition, yet he often failed to breathe life into his lucid and
harmonious forms. His technical resources too far exceeded the requirements of his temperament, and this circumstance, exacerbated by official
ineptitude, made him an unhappy painter.

Dyce studied in Italy, where he acquired a wide understanding of Italian
painting, and came in contact with the Nazarines. After his return to London he was given charge of the Government School of Design (the predecessor of the Royal College of Art). He was involved first as adviser and
later as executant in the project for wall decorations in the Houses of
Parliament, undertaken in 1843. Like everyone else concerned he was
harassed and disappointed. When the young Holman Hunt expressed his
sense of the joy it must be to Dyce to have the opportunity of exercising his
powers on so large a scale on a great State building, he answered sadly, 'But
I begin with my hair already grey.'

There exists at least one painting, however, namely *Pegwell Bay,* in which
Dyce had been so much moved by the memory of a place that his great
resources were brought into full play. It is a representation made with Pre-
Raphaelite precision and Pre-Raphaelite intensity of feeling and with a
practised hand. It is a picture which, once known, haunts the memory with
its delicate autumnal poetry, its poignant identification of the passing of
the day with the passing of life itself. The figure on the right is the painter's
wife; the other ladies are her sisters, Grace and Isabella Brand, the little
boy one of the painter's sons. Donati's Comet, first observed the previous
June, appears in the sky.

WALTER GREAVES 1846–1930
Hammersmith Bridge on Boat-Race Day c. 1862
Canvas 36×55 (91.5×140)

The painter of this picture came of a family of Thames boatmen. His father had rowed Turner, and Walter Greaves (and his brother Harry) used to row Whistler. The brothers also served as his studio assistants, mixing his colours, stretching and priming his canvases and the like. Inevitably the two young boatmen fell deeply under Whistler's spell, and they attempted to substitute for their own direct and richly detailed way of seeing something of his sophistication. He taught them to look for the general shapes of things, and to suppress detail, and the use of his own muted iridescent blue for the rendering of the Thames twilight.

Greaves's relations with Whistler have been insufficiently studied, but their first meeting, although its date has not been precisely established, appears to have taken place in 1863. If this date is correct *Hammersmith Bridge* was painted before Greaves knew Whistler; it shows, at all events, no trace of the characteristics which Whistler recommended. The great bridge pulsates with excited human life seen by eyes avid of detail. The compact unity of the composition, which gives the picture a sophisticated look, is imposed by the iron framework of the bridge itself, whose every horizontal surface is packed with human figures. Its true unity derives not from its iron framework, however, but from what Fry, writing of van Eyck's *Mystic Lamb*, describes as a unity 'essentially poetic and imaginative, and not visual', in this case one communicated by the unity of purpose of the crowd of eager spectators.

A prevailing prejudice disposes many to look for genius not among professionals but among primitives, children and even the insane. The great army of primitives has produced only one master, the Douanier Rousseau, children and lunatics none at all. Had Walter Greaves never been dazzled by Whistler out of his true bent he too might have become a master, for it is difficult to deny a touch of genius to the about sixteen-year-old painter of *Hammersmith Bridge*.

JAMES McNEILL WHISTLER 1834–1903
The Little White Girl ('Symphony in White No. II') 1864
Canvas 30×20 (76×51)

This painting – to be distinguished from *The White Girl* by the same painter, which when it was shown at the *Salon des Refusés* in 1863 provoked a sensation second only to Manet's *Déjeuner sur l'herbe* – represents Jo, for some ten years his favourite model, agent and the centre of his domestic life. Her full name was Joanna Hefferman, and her disreputable old father used to allude to Whistler as 'me son-in-law'. In the winter of 1861 Whistler had taken her to Paris, where Courbet visited them. Admiring her splendid copper-coloured hair, according to Whistler's principal biography, Courbet was moved to make of her the beautiful portrait, now in Stockholm, which he called *La belle Irlandaise*.

The serenity and the distinction of the pose are Whistler's own; the fan, the porcelain and the spray of blossoms are manifestations of the enthusiasm for the art of Japan, then at its height, which had begun some eight years earlier in Paris. Jo's face is represented with a tenderness not often to be seen in Whistler's portraits; in most of them the humanity is subordinated to purely aesthetic considerations, which give them a look that is exquisite but remote. In this picture, painted five years after he settled in London, are to be discovered certain of the elements, the simpler design, the freer handling, which belonged to the great tradition in painting – at that time essentially a French tradition – which Whistler introduced into England.

Swinburne wrote a poem about *The Little White Girl* that took Whistler's fancy; one verse of it runs:

She knows not loves that kissed her,
She knows not where
Art thou the ghost my sister,
White sister there,
Am I the ghost, who knows?
My hand, a fallen rose,
Lies snow-white on white snows, and takes no care.

JOHN S. SARGENT 1856–1925
Vernon Lee 1881
Canvas 20¹/₂×16 (52×41)

The painter of the portrait reproduced here was born more than a century
ago, but posterity has not yet assigned to him any secure place in the
hierarchy of painters of his time. For the latter half of his life and during
the years immediately following his death he was treated with adulation by
the majority of critics. During all this time the earnest minority allowed
him – beyond his virtuosity which was indeed too conspicuous to be denied –
scarcely any virtues, and pronounced him flashy and superficial: a thoroughly
able servant of mammon. Of recent years, except by his fellow countrymen
(though resident in London he remained a citizen of the United States), he
has been accorded little notice, favourable or the reverse.

A servant of mammon in some sort he was, for fashionable portraiture
involves a measure of compromise between the painter's view of his sitter
and the view of himself (or herself) which the sitter commissions him to
perpetuate. Sargent, the most successful portrait painter of his time, a man
moreover of determined character and impressive presence, made the mini-
mum of concessions. Indeed the way in which this puritanical and unmerce-
nary painter could make shocking revelations about the rapacity and vul-
garity of his sitters and calmly pocket the price was a source of amusement
to his friends. The truth seems to be that Sargent was uninterested in the
psychology of his sitters, and his revelations were the result of a combination of a preternaturally penetrating eye and a gifted hand. He was a
superficial draughtsman, an uninteresting colourist, traditionless and worldly
in his outlook, but his marvellous – if unconscious – insight into character
enabled him to paint portraits worthy to stand beside those of his fellow
expatriate Henry James. 'Vernon Lee' – the pen-name of Violet Paget – was
a friend, and the author, incidentally, of the most comprehending study yet
written of the painter: the revelations he makes about her concern her acute
intelligence and her sensibility.

PHILIP WILSON STEER 1860–1942
Girls Running: Walberswick Pier 1894
Canvas 24¹/₂✕36¹/₂ (62✕93)

Until about the early nineteen-forties Steer enjoyed a discreet illustriousness
as the foremost successor, in his oil paintings, of Constable, and in his water-
colours, of Turner. Although he was without the sonority or the freshness
of the one or the lofty and abundant genius of the other (he was a modest
man and it would not have occurred to him to acknowledge a claim to
either), he was a painter who had to his credit a long series of landscapes
which showed that he was indeed no unworthy successor of these two great
masters.

The best of his opulent summary landscapes were often of a noble character, but their nobility was apt to be softened by a vitiating hint of languid
complacency. Rather less than twenty years ago a certain phase of his earlier
work began to be rediscovered – a phase which his most ardent advocates
discounted when they did not ignore it. These were a series of figures in
landscape sharply distinct from those to which he owed his fame. Of this
series the finest is the picture here reproduced. There is no hint of complacency about the two intent, lanky young girls running quickly away
from the sea along a pier. The composition is unremarkable; the figures have
little form or substance, yet there they are, animated by an odd, disturbing
energy, racing towards us across the wide planks, the white broad-sashed,
rather formal dresses touched with the glory of the day. They are strange
girls, and why are they running so fast?

If Renoir had painted the picture, the effect might have been of greater
breadth and radiance; had Lautrec, the strangeness of the girls might have
been explained; yet as it is there is a freshness, an immediacy, an angular,
unsophisticated grace which, manifest in every inch of the picture's surface,
make it memorable.

WALTER RICHARD SICKERT 1860–1942
The Interior of St Mark's, Venice 1901–3
Canvas 26^7/$_8$ × 18^5/$_8$ (68 × 47)

In recoil from the tastefulness and elegance of his master Whistler – qualities
which he came to regard as art's most insidious enemies – Sickert sought his
subjects in the kitchen instead of the drawing-room, and handsome landscape subjects he disparaged as 'august sites'. The picture here reproduced
is the representation of just such a site.

Sickert went to Venice for the first time in 1895 and again in the winters
of 1901 and 1903. 'On cold days', he wrote to his friend Steer, 'I do interiors in St Mark's.' 'It may be a poor compliment,' the letter continues,
'but for all practical purposes, the more experience I have the more I find
that the only things that seem to me to have a direct bearing on the practical purpose of painting are the things I have learnt from you. To see the
thing all at once. To work open and loose, freely . . .' Sickert went into
St Mark's to paint it because the weather was cold along the canals, and he
did not exploit the architectural beauty of this fabulous basilica. Essentially
he was an Impressionist – an Impressionist with a difference in that he was
concerned with the lower rather than the upper register of tone – but a true
Impressionist in that he saw form in terms of colour. If he ignored the
picturesque strangeness of the Byzantine interior, he was alive to the play
of the gold, the green and the blue light from the mosaics as at points they
glow in the prevailing gloom. Sickert's observation delights at once by its
truth and by the unexpected, the epigrammatic, way in which the truth is
stated.

AUGUSTUS JOHN 1878–1961
Robin c. 1909
Canvas 18×14 (46×36)

Only rarely is there an artist whose response to faces is so lively and sustained as to enable him to make it his entire profession, and he who paints nothing except portraits deadens his response. This is no doubt the principal reason why most of the memorable portraits of modern times are not the work of professionals but of painters who renew the vivacity of their response to faces by change of subject. In spite of the number of portraits Augustus John painted, his constant preoccupation with figure drawings, landscapes, flower-pieces and most of all with big figure compositions or studies for them, enabled him to retain his amateur standing.

Robin, a likeness of one of his sons, shows him at his finest. Noble form, built up by strokes of the brush which are swift but unerring, and radiant colour combine in the making of an image which has the troubled look, the glowing health, the pent-up energy that makes it live not simply as a likeness but as an independent creation.

122

SIR MATTHEW SMITH, 1879–1960
Apples on a Dish 1919
Canvas 18 × 21¹/₂ (46 × 55)

It was not until about 1914, when Matthew Smith was in his middle thirties, that his tentative art attained a sudden, aggressive maturity and he began to paint with a passionate opulence of colour and form: the effect, perhaps, of revulsion from the twilight grimness of industrial Yorkshire where he was born and brought up, of exultation at having completed a protracted and unhappy apprenticeship, and of his brief but exhilarating attendance at the school in Paris where Matisse taught.

In this painting Matthew Smith has followed the injunction of the dying Crome to his son to dignify whatever he painted, and his apples have a nobility of form and, fused with it, colour that is both audacious and delicately astringent. The fusion, however, is not quite complete: the picture has something of the character of a powerful coloured drawing. In his later paintings colour and form are still more intimately fused: form and space are stated entirely in terms of colour.

HAROLD GILMAN 1878–1919
Mrs Mounter at the Breakfast Table 1916
Canvas 23¹/₂×15¹/₂ (59×39)

Cézanne, van Gogh, Gauguin and Seurat were all several years dead by the time that the effects of the transformation of French painting became widely felt in England. Their work was known, of course, to a number of individual painters, but it was not until the exhibition organized in 1910 by Roger Fry, 'Manet and the Post-Impressionists', that British artists as a whole came to appreciate and to be affected by the revolutionary ferment.

Among the painters whom this impact moved to reconsider the basic principles of their art was Harold Gilman who, beginning as a disciple of Velazquez and Whistler, had shortly before this momentous exhibition been led to an enhanced sense of the attractions of the pure and brilliant colour of the Impressionists. He now determined to retain their colour, but to reject the Impressionist conception of painting as having the character of a random sketch, made under an ephemeral effect of light, and to give his own work the character of permanence and dignity. Gilman confided to a friend that one of his greatest ambitions was to seize the essence of a character and exhibit it on canvas in all its bearings. This he achieved in his portraits of his charlady, Mrs Mounter, of which the larger version is at Liverpool and the small preliminary study is the version reproduced here. Their majestic design in broad planes, resonant colour and tender insight place them among the finest English portraits of their time.

PAUL NASH 1889–1946
Pillar and Moon 1932–42
Canvas 20×30 (51×76)

As a young man Paul Nash served first as a soldier, later as an Official War Artist, on the Western Front in the First World War. It is not too much to say that it was this terrible experience that made him an artist. Out of the huge prospect of devastation, of earth burnt or dissolved into an oily poisoned swamp, of elms, oaks, beeches blasted into anonymous stumps, he realized an apocalyptic vision. When the war ended and he no longer had this overwhelming theatre of action to exact his spirit, to engage to the utmost all his powers, he was deeply aware of the void it left: 'a war artist without a war' was how he described himself. The remainder of his life was spent largely in the search for subjects to which he could respond with comparable exaltation. Towards the end of it he was moved by imaginings of forms evocative of the interplay of vaguely elemental and mysterious forces.

Of the series of pictures to which this one belongs he wrote that 'the idea behind the design is the mystical association of two objects which inhabit different elements and have no apparent relation to life'. In *Pillar and Moon* the pale stone sphere on top of a ruined pillar faces its counterpart, the moon, cold and pale and solid as stone. No legend or history attaches to such a picture, its drama is inherent in the scene. Its appeal is purely evocatory. That is to say, its power, if power it has, is to call up memories and stir emotions in the spectator, rather than to impose a particular idea upon him. Even so the animation of such a picture lies in its ruling design. Not only does this dictate the nature of the drama; it also expresses by its forms and colours the nature of its mystery.

SIR STANLEY SPENCER, 1891–1959
The Resurrection, Cookham 1923–7   Canvas 108×216 (274×549)

The theme of the Resurrection obsessed Spencer for the greater part of his life. As long ago as 1913 he made two small paintings of it, and thereafter he painted three further *Resurrections* on a great scale: the painting here reproduced; *The Resurrection of Soldiers, Macedonia*, of 1928–9; and *The Resurrection, Port Glasgow*, of 1945–50. Spencer's concept of his theme had undergone radical change since he first attempted it. In the two early *Resurrections of Good and Bad* it conforms to the scriptural conception: the 'good' are shown as radiant and the 'bad' as despairing.

In that of 1928–9, perhaps the greatest religious wall painting made in England since the Reformation – scores of soldiers contemplate their crosses, and in the growing realization that they share in the Crucifixion of Christ welcome and embrace them. In the last he has abandoned the scriptural

interpretation: the 'good' and 'bad' are not separated, nor indeed distinguished; there is no intimation of an impending Judgment. Spencer was deeply
attached to his native place, the Thames-side village of Cookham. The
setting of *The Resurrection, Cookham* is the churchyard with the Thames
in the background. God the Father and Christ with the little children are
seen under the porch in the centre. The artist is represented reclining on a
tombstone in the bottom right-hand corner, and again, naked, head in
profile to the right, close to the porch, and Hilda, his first wife, lies in the
overgrown grave in the centre foreground, and she appears again on the
left smelling a flower. A vague sense that the events in the Bible had been
and were enacted in the region where he was born early took a hold upon
Spencer's imagination. There is no ground for supposing that there was in
his mind anything approaching an explicit identification of these Islands
with the New Jerusalem, but he was free from the widely current heresy
according to which the Christian religion belongs irrevocably to the past.

BEN NICHOLSON b. 1894
Painting 1937
Canvas 62³/₄×79¹/₄ (159.5×201)

When the history of the art of the first half of the twentieth century comes to be written, Abstraction may well seem to have been its most characteristic form. Should this prove to be the case, the work here reproduced will have a double value, as a work of great distinction in its own right and as a work of exceptional historical interest. It manifests in a high degree the precise and subtle understanding of the relations between forms of this artist at his happiest, and his capacity for making a significant work of art out of the simplest elements. Historically, it represents an important, perhaps the dominant, style of the age in its extremest form. Subject, tone, atmosphere, movement are excluded, and, of course, all recognizable reference to the world of normal vision – almost every one of those elements, in fact, out of which, from the cave-men to the Surrealists, artists have made their pictures.

Ben Nicholson is widely acclaimed, not in his own country alone, as the most accomplished living exponent of abstract art. He does not, however, belong to the race of pioneers: abstract art had already been brought to maturity by the time he came to practise it, by Kandinsky, Brancusi, Mondrian, Arp and others, but no one has ever brought to it so precise a sense of perfection as he.

Nicholson has produced works of a less abstract character, including clearly recognizable representations of landscapes and ordinary household objects. The Tate possesses six other examples of his work.

GRAHAM SUTHERLAND b. 1903
Entrance to a Lane 1939
Canvas 23¹/₂×19¹/₂ (60×50)

The picture here reproduced is one of a group belonging to Sutherland's remarkable first years as a painter. When he began to paint he was in no sense a beginner as an artist: his vision, nourished by the English imaginative tradition, in particular by Blake and Samuel Palmer, had expressed itself in a series of etchings and drawings which at first seem to be the work of an artist firmly rooted in a romantic pastoral tradition but under scrutiny yield evidence of the more violent, even the more cruel, way of apprehending the world apparent in the later phases of his art. Around 1936, when he first visited Pembrokeshire, he was fully prepared to profit by the experience afforded by the sight of its rugged landscape. 'It was in this country', he wrote in a letter to a friend, 'that I began to learn painting.' The most revealing phrase in a revealing piece of writing is: 'I found I could express what I felt only by paraphrasing what I saw.' The effect of his experience in Pembrokeshire seems to have been to clarify his ideas and to complete his liberation from a dependence upon his early masters which if too long continued would have hampered his growth. It was as though he moved out of their orbit and towards that of Picasso. The places which have most readily provided the harsh and sometimes tortured paraphrases, or equivalents, rocks, fallen trees, thorns, spiky vegetation, for Sutherland's thought and feeling, besides Pembrokeshire, are Cornwall and Provence.

Entrance to a Lane was painted from drawings made in Pembrokeshire. The Tate owns sixteen works by this artist, including two other early landscapes, *Welsh Landscape*, of 1937 and *Green Tree Form: Interior of Woods*, of 1939.

JOHN PIPER b. 1903
Somerset Place, Bath 1942
Water-colour 18×29 (46×74)

In 1934 Piper, who had painted in a variety of styles, turned to Abstraction. Three years later he published a lively and significant article entitled 'Lost, a valuable Object', in which he contends that 'artists everywhere have done their best to find something to replace the object that Cubism destroyed. ... They have been frantic and calm by turns. They have adopted simple means, and very complicated ones,' and he frankly declared his own nostalgia for it and his faith in its reappearance. The artist expressed himself more effectively as an abstract painter than those acquainted only with his work in other styles might suppose, but it was inevitable that a man fascinated by so many of the activities of man – in particular by the buildings he erects for his habitation, his worship, his government or his pleasure – should feel the constriction of so uncommunicative a style. During the later 'thirties the subject, accordingly, 'kept breaking in', but the full realization of his nostalgia came in an unexpected and horrifying form: the second World War.

Even as a boy Piper explored country churches, making rubbings from brasses and tracings of stained glass, and on holidays abroad making drawings of architecture, and since then his interest in architecture and in landscape which bears the impress of man's activity has broadened and intensified. Then, at a moment when the expression of these interests was still confined by Abstraction, the war came, and the buildings that he had studied and delighted in were ravaged and destroyed by the thousand. His appointment in 1942 as an Official War Artist gave him an opportunity, or rather placed him under an obligation, to record his horror at the desecration that daily, nightly, was overwhelming the things which meant most to him. He responded with vehemence, and a sense of drama that had scarcely hitherto been a feature of his work became its dominant feature. Incidentally it was the sense of drama generated by the war that made Piper one of the foremost designers for the theatre.

The picture here reproduced is one of those which he made as an Official War Artist.

The Tate also owns nine other examples, including an abstract painting, of the work of one of the most versatile artists now alive and the creator of a style at once highly personal and so compendious as to assimilate influences as diverse as Picasso and the architecture of Welsh Nonconformity.

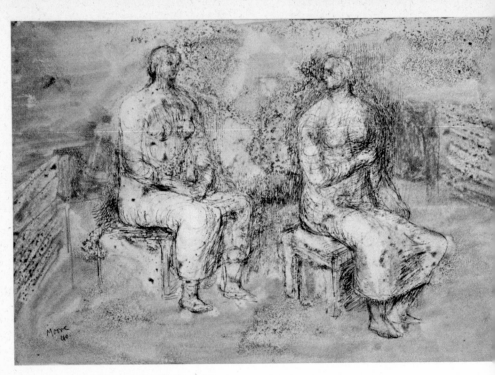

HENRY MOORE b. 1898
Two Seated Women 1940
Pen and ink, water-colour and chalk 9×10⁵/₈ (23×27)

This drawing was made very shortly before the shelter drawings, and it serves both as an intimation of the impending change of direction in the work of Henry Moore, and as an illustration of the radical nature of it. Compared with earlier drawings *Two Seated Women* expressed a tender sentiment, but compared with the shelter drawings this sentiment is tentative and diffuse, expressed rather in the delicacy of the colour than in the treatment of the figures.

The medium used in this picture—pen and ink, water-colour and chalk—is now used so widely that it is forgotten that the combination is an invention of Moore's—an invention made not long before this drawing. Shortly before the outbreak of the Second World War, a niece asked him to make her a drawing, and obligingly supplied her own materials, a few cheap crayons and some water-colours. It was in the doing of this kindly act that he discovered the method, which he has constantly used, of putting in the main masses with a white wax crayon.

136

VICTOR PASMORE b. 1908
Spiral Motif in Green, Violet, Blue and Gold.
The Coast of the Inland Sea 1950   Canvas 32 × 39¹/₂ (81 × 100)

About twenty years ago a critic wrote of the artistic temper of Victor
Pasmore 'it is that of one who paints as a bird sings rather than as an
architect builds. So joyfully, so unscientifically . . . does he pursue his theme
. . . Pasmore paints because he loves painting.' How consistently justified by
a considerable body of work that opinion seemed. At that time Pasmore
was thirty, and already he seemed to have a secure place in a tradition
stemming from Degas, and in temperament this born painter seemed to be
closer to Whistler than to anyone else, and next to Bonnard.

Yet within a few years Pasmore had become a painter of abstractions
such as the painting reproduced here – which still gave scope to his gifts for
colour and design but involved the abandonment of everything that seemed
to be most quintessentially his own. A few years later still he had virtually
abandoned painting in favour of abstract designs made in plastic. His career
is a testimony to the attraction of the *Zeitgeist* in the form of that recoil
from nature of which the logical consequence is abstract art.

LUCIAN FREUD b. 1922
Francis Bacon 1952
Oil on copper 7×5 (18×13)

The art of some painters is the product of imagination, of others of 'the moment of vision', of others again of the synthesis of different impressions of the same subject, or of a combination of two or even all three of these processes. The art of Lucian Freud is the product of a long unblinking stare – a stare without warmth, without illusion, a stare above all of sheer fascination. Freud is intensely curious about the object of his stare, coolly determined to penetrate its secret life, yet not content humbly to place on record what he perceives; he is impelled to impose something of himself on the object of his hypnotic observation. Were he content merely to record, his work would be pedestrian; if simply to impose, it would lack veracity. It is the tension between the urge towards scrupulous observation in him and the urge to impose himself that gives his painting its unique character. The disquieting stillness which is the most conspicuous attribute of the work of Freud is the product of equilibrium between conflicting forces.

MODERN FOREIGN SCHOOL

VINCENT VAN GOGH 1853–90
La Chaise et la Pipe 1888–9
Canvas 36³/₄×29 (93.5×73.5)

This painting, made in Arles some eighteen months before the painter's death, is one of a pair. It represents his own empty chair; its companion, painted at the same time, represents that of Gauguin. The subjects of many of van Gogh's pictures represent personal experiences – personal experiences distinct from the delight aroused by their visual qualities. He was charged with a passionate sympathy not only for the whole of nature but also for the commonplace objects of his daily use, which for him were often special revelations of the meaning of life. One scholar has expressed the opinion that many of his realistic subjects really represent private cryptograms. There are reasons for presuming this to be the case in the present instance. In a letter to his brother (no. 252) Vincent wrote '*Edwin Drood* was Dicken's last work, and Luke Fildes, brought into contact with Dickens through those small illustrations, enters his room on the day of his death, sees his empty chair standing there, and so it happens that one of the old numbers of *The Graphic* contains that touching drawing: *The Empty Chair*.'

The two chair paintings were painted not long before the terrible events which were to put an end to his troubled friendship with Gauguin and to precipitate van Gogh's own journey into a nightmare world. The paintings are clear premonitions of impending tragedy; of his own death and his quarrel with Gauguin. One of his earlier paintings represented a chair, the chair of his dead father. It would of course be an error to think of such paintings as these only as symbols: van Gogh may have been a literary painter, but he was an impassioned painter. 'In these two studies,' he wrote, 'I have tried for an effect of light by means of pure colour.' For all his vehemence van Gogh knew how to create forms perfectly adapted to the ideas which he needed so urgently to communicate.

HENRI DE TOULOUSE-LAUTREC 1864–1901
Les Deux Amies 1894
Oil on millboard 18⁷/₈×13³/₈ (48×35)

Living creatures–in his earlier days dogs and horses, his fellow human
beings later on–were the subjects of the art of Lautrec. 'Nothing exists but
the figure', he declared. Landscape and interiors concerned him only in so
far as they served to explain figures or character. And he preferred his
living creatures in action. His method of work was to make lightning
sketches, which formed the foundation of his art. But in order to preserve
in the oil paintings which he made from them the impression of action
recorded on the spot he evolved a style that had much of the character of
the sketch. Detail irrelevant to his purpose was omitted, his line was
economical but sharply expressive, the paint was hatched on with rapid
strokes.

Lautrec sought his subjects occasionally in operating theatre and law
court but mainly in the places which they frequented for pleasure: circus,
racecourse, dance-hall, music-hall and brothel. The painting here reproduced is one of the famous series he made of Parisian brothels. Into these
houses he would disappear for days at a time, where, instead of the conventional professional model of the studios, he could observe girls moving
about, dressing and undressing, unconscious of or indifferent to observation,
and he delighted in recording their casual, uninhibited poses and gestures.
There is nothing sordid in Lautrec's treatment of such subjects. His brothel
paintings are worthy expressions of his attitude towards his fellow creatures:
he observed them through ruthless eyes that overlooked none of their im-
perfections either of body or of mind; yet he did not judge them or even
abate the affection in which he held them: that is the measure of Lautrec's
humanity.

PAUL GAUGUIN 1848–1903
Faa Iheihe 1898   Canvas 21¹/₄×66¹/₂ (54×169)

The formality of its pattern of rich colours and the untroubled exoticism
which pervades it might persuade a person to whom the life and ideas of
Gauguin were unknown that the intention behind the picture here reproduced was purely decorative. Indeed this and other paintings made by
Gauguin in Oceania have inspired many imitations prompted by just such
an intention. Even one to whom the artist is not unknown, seeing this picture
on a wall at the Tate, is apt to forget the heroic purposefulness in conditions
of the utmost suffering in which it came into being on a remote island in
the Pacific. Gauguin had a conspicuous talent for decoration, but decoration
as an end in itself would neither have engaged his powerful intellect nor
justified the terrible ordeal he endured in order to pursue his art.

No contrast could be more extreme than the contrast between Gauguin
and Watts: Gauguin – revolutionary in vision, heroically independent and
adventurous in his life; Watts – content in the Greco-Roman tradition, timid
and pampered in his life. Yet in one important respect their aims were

strikingly similar. Both were deeply and increasingly aware of the corrupting effects of a special kind of materialism upon the spiritual life of Western society. It impelled both to preach, in pictures in every other way dissimilar, against the evils which they believed were eroding and, unchecked, would eventually destroy, the fabric of civilization. Watts spent his life in relative isolation in the company of chosen spirits; but Gauguin sought rejuvenation and subjects for his art among primitive peoples, in Brittany, Martinique and eventually in Tahiti and the Marquesas, and he gradually evolved an eloquent language of simplified, almost hieratic, forms and pure, strong colours.

Faa Iheihe, which means decoration and is less charged than most of his works with philosophic overtones, was painted in Tahiti at a time of culminating personal tragedy for Gauguin: his daughter Aline had died; he was ill and almost starving, compelled to move away from his hut, and he had attempted to kill himself with a dose of arsenic. It is a fine painting, but overshadowed by *Whence do we come; what are we; whither are we going?* – with which it has close stylistic affinities – a last attempt to paint a great picture, an allegory of life and death.

EDGAR DEGAS 1834–1917
Femme à sa Toilette c. 1894
Pastel 37⅝×43¼ (95.5×110)

With increasing years painters incline to see their subjects more broadly
and to treat them more loosely. The names of Titian, Rembrandt, Gainsborough, Turner and Corot come instantly to mind as conspicuously sharing
this inclination. Also that of Degas. But increasing years are also apt to
bring to most painters except the greatest an inclination towards caution,
towards the repetition of past successes. Such an inclination Degas was far
from sharing: the latter half of his life was the time when he showed himself most daring in experiment. In his earlier work his line was precise –
he was an ardent admirer of Ingres – and his colour suave in tone and
smoothly applied. In the middle of his life his eyesight began to fail, but
instead of despairing he had the courage and resource to make what for
another would have been disaster the occasion for changing his methods so
as to enable him to express himself with enhanced originality. From the
'eighties, pastel (which until some ten years previously he had regarded as
a secondary medium) became the medium he used for most of his principal
pictures. Gradually Degas evolved a method, or rather a wide variety of
methods, which enabled him to use pastel with an expressive force with
which it had never been used before. He compensated for his inability to
draw with his former meticulous precision with greater audacity of composition, and with richer and more vibrant colour. These late pastels give
the impression, because of their immediacy, of having been made from life:
they were made in fact from careful preparatory studies. The picture here
reproduced is one of these late pastels in which he sought to represent above
all vigorous yet unselfconscious action. To heighten the illusion of such
action surprised, as it were, by a camera-shot, he often cut figures – in this
instance the servant with the cup – with his picture edge.

PABLO PICASSO b. 1881
Femme en Chemise c. 1905
Canvas 28³/₄ × 23³/₈ (73 × 59.5)

No painter of comparable stature has ever been so various as Picasso. One phase of his art has followed upon another so quickly – some of them lasted no longer than a few months–that it is difficult to discern not only the Picasso of the moment but even the enduring features of his personality. Such a degree of changefulness as his creative life exhibits is a rare phenomenon. Most artists are obsessed with a few themes and a logically evolving style. Faced with the picture reproduced here, that discussed on the following page, painted only some four years later, and, say *Guernica,* a student of some remote period in the future who knew nothing of Picasso might well fail to perceive anything in common between them.

1905, the year when *Femme en Chemise* was painted, was the year when Fauvism erupted in the face of an angry public, to remain for some years the focus of interest for advanced painters. Oblivious of its struggle for a new, more immediate and more forceful means of expression in terms of brusque, summary forms and pure, violent colours, Picasso continued to paint pictures which had more in common with those of Puvis de Chavannes, Rossetti and even Burne-Jones than with those of his radical contemporaries with whom he was to make a break with tradition that was without precedent for its violence in the entire history of European art. There is nothing in the gentle, dreamy figures of the period of Picasso's art to which this picture belongs, by no means invariably free from a quite commonplace sentimentality for the self-conscious 'decadence' of the previous decade, to foreshadow the ferocious dynamism, the satiric humour, the restlessness, the endless inventiveness which, among other qualities, were to make Picasso's creative life the most continuously revolutionary that the twentieth century has so far to show.

PABLO PICASSO b. 1881
Seated Nude 1909–10
Oil on canvas 36¹/₄×28³/₄ (92×73)

This painting, representing a woman in a high-backed chair, is one of the outstanding examples of the Analytical Cubism practised by Picasso and Braque between 1909 and 1912.

A curious feature of the Cubism of this period is that while it has come to be increasingly regarded as an expression of one of the great moments in the painting of the century – 'heroic' is a term often used to describe it – there still remains a diversity of opinion about its essential character. By some it is regarded as an extreme revolutionary movement, by others as a recall to classical severity and precision. There is, however, a wide measure of agreement as to its derivation from Cézanne, in particular from his injunction to discern solid geometrical forms beneath the flux of appearance. But the singularity has been noted that although Cézanne cites the cylinder, the sphere and the cone he made no mention of the cube from which the movement takes its name.

Analytical Cubism has something of the character of an investigation of natural phenomena and of their taking apart, for the purpose of making a new language of form. It is also distinguished by sombre, muted colour and a relative absence of recession. Whatever its essential it can scarcely be denied that its finest products continue to impose themselves upon our consciousness with an ever-growing authority.

ANDRE DERAIN 1880–1954
The Pool of London 1906
Canvas 25⁷/₈×39 (66×99)

Of the series of revolutionary movements which completed the radical transformation of painting begun by Cézanne, Gauguin, van Gogh and Seurat, perhaps the most radical was Fauvism, which came to the notice of the public in the autumn of 1905. It was an impatient and violent movement: the Fauves aimed at a simpler and more direct mode of expression than the elaborate procedures of earlier painters allowed, and they accordingly effected a drastic simplification of their technical methods. They assigned to colour an independent function and they attempted to lighten its descriptive burden. Matisse, who was rightly described as 'The King of the Fauves', had met Derain in 1899 or thereabouts at the Académie Carrière, and Derain had introduced him to Vlaminck at the van Gogh exhibition of 1901. Fauvism had serious limitations: it offered no means of conveying fine shades of meaning, nor of satisfying the desire of twentieth-century painters for structure. It was too vehement, too crude, to satisfy its originators for long. In the course of its ephemeral life the energy and the candour of the Fauves enabled them, however, to paint a number of memorable pictures: the harsh vehemence with which these proclaim, in terms of pure, brilliant colour, certain uncomplicated facts about nature, and, of course, about their creators' preoccupations, makes an enduring impression on their beholders.

After a visit to London, Vollard, the famous dealer, was deeply impressed by the pictorial possibilities of the city's atmosphere and wanted pictures in which Monet's brilliant successes in its interpretation would be repeated in contemporary terms. He accordingly sent Derain to London, where he worked in 1905, 1906, 1907 and 1910. The painting here reproduced, which would seem to have been made from London Bridge, is among the finest of the group of London scenes – mostly along the Thames ('The Thames is immense' he wrote) although he also worked in Regent Street and Hyde Park – which he painted for Vollard. It is strange to remember that the last of Monet's London pictures were painted only a year before the first of Derain's; yet even though Derain had evidently studied Monet the two series belong to ages utterly remote from each other.

EDVARD MUNCH 1863–1944
The Sick Child 1906–7
Canvas 46³/₄×47⁵/₈ (119×121)

An older painter, by way of expressing his disappointment at the direction
that Munch's art had taken, said to him: 'I didn't think that was the kind
of painting you were going to do.' 'Well,' replied Munch, 'everybody can't
be painting nails and twigs.' Munch was certainly no painter of nails and
twigs, or of any ordinary things. He was a painter of life intensified – often
to the point of frenzy – by strong emotions, most often fear and sex, and
often the two combined. As a young man he himself suffered from a scarcely
endurable dread of life, and he recoiled violently from the hypocrisy with
which sex was treated by the respectable society of his time.

As an old man Munch still spoke with emotion of his unhappy childhood. His father 'suffered from periods of religious anxiety which could
reach the verge of insanity . . .' 'Disease and insanity were the black angels
on guard at my cradle . . . I felt always that I was treated in an unjust way,
without a mother, sick, and with threatened punishment in Hell hanging
over my head.' The terrors of his childhood continued, then, to haunt his
imagination and to furnish motives for his art. The picture here reproduced
– he made five other versions in oils and three prints of the subject – is
supposed to have been inspired by the death of his elder sister Sophie who
died in 1877 from the tuberculosis that had also killed his mother. Unlike
the girl in the picture, Sophie appears not to have had red hair. The subject,
therefore, may represent the fusion of two memories. According to the
artist the several versions 'were unlike each other and each makes its special
contribution to the first impression' of 'the sick child – the pale head with
the very red hair against the white pillow'. The first version of the picture
he regarded as 'opening a new path. It was a breakthrough in my art. Most
of what I have done later had its birth in this picture.'

Munch was one of the artists whose works were condemned by Hitler as
'degenerate art', and all his works from German museums – including this
picture, then in the Dresden Gallery – were sold to foreign dealers in 1938.

GEORGES ROUAULT 1871–1958
Têtes à Massacre ('Aunt Sallies') 1907
Oil on paper, mounted on canvas 29¹/₂×41¹/₂ (75×105.5)

All artists owe much to the examples of predecessors and contemporaries, but among the painters of the twentieth century few occupy so solitary a position as Rouault. The art of almost all his contemporaries, whether realist or abstract, is aesthetic in intention. The art of Rouault is religious: he was a painter of sin and redemption. Sin and redemption are the veritable subjects of his pictures, not subjects chosen because of the dramatic, aesthetic or archaeological possibilities they offer. Yet no one less resembles the stock 'religious' painter. He is ferocious: he believes it to be a duty of art to represent evil as ugly (as it is, if not on the surface, only just beneath). 'If art does not go on its knees ... it must necessarily go on its back or its belly.' This saying, which was often on Rouault's lips, comes from the writings of his friend Léon Bloy, who with other late nineteenth-century Catholic writers has contributed so largely to the formation of his intellect. The style of Rouault is as individual as his thinking. The artist himself has told us that he 'went first to school with Daumier' (there were a number of his lithographs in his grandfather's house) before knowing Raphael, and no doubt the Fauves contributed towards the Expressionism of his style, although his own spiritual and intellectual Expressionism contrasted sharply with the aesthetic Expressionism of Matisse, Derain, Vlaminck and the other Fauves. The painting here reproduced was formerly known as *La Mariée (The Bride)*, although it was originally exhibited as *La Mariée (Fantoches) (Puppets)*. In 1953 Rouault asked the Gallery to change the title to that at the head of this note. The Aunt Sallies represent perhaps satiric reflections on the corruption of Fallen Man.

MAURICE UTRILLO 1883–1955
La Porte St Martin c. 1911
Oil on millboard 27¹/₄×31¹/₂ (69×80)

In earlier periods it was believed that there existed certain definite canons and that works of art were great in so far as they conformed to them. It followed that works of art were great in so far as they resembled acknowledged masterpieces, that there was in fact a sort of family resemblance between masterpieces. Of late it has come to be believed, on the contrary, that great works of art are unique, and even that they are great in proportion to their uniqueness. Today, when traditions dissolve and personality asserts itself as never before, it is the latter hypothesis that seems to us to do better justice to the facts.

The painter of the picture here reproduced is unlikely ever to be ranked among the masters, but he was a considerable painter, and almost everything about him and his methods is in contradiction with the accepted notions of a serious artist.

Utrillo had no innate desire to be a painter, in spite of the example of his mother, Suzanne Valadon. As a schoolboy he formed a craving for alcohol, even for absinthe, which he seems to have done nothing to restrain. The family doctor first suggested that purely for therapeutic purposes a pencil should be placed in his hands. Suzanne Valadon followed his advice, which her son received badly, but she persisted, and it was only after obstinate resistance that he took up painting, although eventually with passion.

The most precious quality in the painting of Utrillo is his extraordinary sensibility to the character of places, a sensibility that seems the more remarkable when we remember that Utrillo usually painted the same places, Montmartre and a few other areas in or just outside Paris, and more astonishing still when we recall the fact–in the presence of his works so easy to forget–that during the greater part of his life as a painter his landscapes were made from postcards. (His principal biographer has stated that from the end of 1909 he became less and less able to paint without their help.) *La Porte St Martin,* which represents a triumphal arch erected in Paris in 1674, shows a view from the middle of a street and seems to have been painted from a postcard.

JUAN GRIS 1887–1927
La Jalousie 1914
Papier collé on canvas, with some heightening in charcoal
36¹/₄×28⁵/₈ (92×72.5)

The style of Gris was principally formed by Cubism, perhaps the most original and fruitful movement in modern art, yet he was not an innovator. His aim was to perfect his own very personal form of Cubism, and he disapproved of what he stigmatized as the exaggerations of the innovating art of his time. Indeed he thought of himself as a somewhat solitary classical temperament among a generation ready to welcome disorder and with an aversion from discipline and clarity. In particular he disliked abstract art as an art unconcerned with reality, and Dadaism and Expressionism as discrediting the real achievements of the time. In short he regarded himself as in essentials a traditional painter, contemporary and personal in vision, but in method a follower of the old masters.

For Gris painting was an art of flat, coloured forms. Forms too solidly modelled seemed to him more the business of the sculptor than of the painter. It was an art from which it was necessary to exclude 'illusionism', that is to say the imitation of natural objects, especially by chiaroscuro. It was necessary to 'create' objects on canvas or paper, but not to 'imitate'; and it was permitted to incorporate, on canvas, a fragment of mirror or, as in the picture here reproduced, a clipping from a newspaper, as contributions to the 'honesty' of the representation and to a certain impersonality at which he aimed. The newspaper, as it happens, was that which circulated in Collioure where the picture was painted. *The Sunblind* finely illustrates the highly developed sense of harmony and the luminous lucidity that distinguish the art of Gris, one of the masters of modern painting who feared that painting was losing its way.

MARC CHAGALL b. 1887
Le Poète Allongé 1915
Oil on millboard 30³/₈ × 30¹/₂ (77 × 77.5)

Like Constable and Wordsworth Chagall was one of those who gathered in
their youth the greater part of the material of their art. He was born in
Vitebsk, Russia, a small provincial and largely Jewish city, of a devout
Jewish family, and his early memories were coloured by ritual and dated
by fasts and feasts. In spite of many difficulties he began to paint, and his
first important picture, *Candles in the Dark Street*, painted when he was
nineteen, set the pattern for his life's work. As is often the case the element
of invention plays a smaller and fact a larger part in the creation of a work
of art than might be supposed: both the dead man, stretched out on the
ground, his face lighted by six candles, and the old man on the roof derive
from Chagall's memory rather than from his imagination. Towards the end
of 1910 he moved to Paris. Here the bright colours, the solemn ritual, the
sad pleasures and the constantly impending tragedy of the Jewish com-
munity in the little town where he was born all burned with trance bright-
ness in his memory. And here the creative ferment affected him as a liberat-
ing and vivifying force. The life of Vitebsk was recreated on his canvases
with a rich fantasy touched by sad humour. Although his art was enriched
and disciplined by the creative ferment of Paris, he was uninterested by
Parisian artists' preoccupations with formal problems; with means, that is
to say, rather than ends. As he once explained to Apollinaire, Impressionism, Symbolism, Cubism, seemed to him only so much formal baggage.

In 1914 he returned to Vitebsk for what he intended as no more than a
visit, but the First World War immediately broke out and it was almost
nine years before he was able to get back to Paris. This experience had a
distinct effect upon his painting. During four years in Paris Vitebsk had
lived with an exuberant fantasy in his imagination. Suddenly confronted
with the substance of his dreams he felt no compulsion to remember or to
imagine, but simply to record. The paintings he made during the first part
of his visit to Russia were accordingly more precise and less exuberant than
those he had made in Paris. The painting here reproduced was painted in
Russia during the honeymoon following his first marriage. Of the days after
the marriage he wrote in his autobiography: 'At last we are alone in the
country. Woods, pines, solitude. The moon behind the forest. The pig in the
sty, the horse behind the window, in the fields. The sky lilac.'

HENRI MATISSE 1869–1954
Arbre près de l'Étang de Trivaux c. 1916
Canvas 36$^{1}/_{2}$×29$^{1}/_{4}$ (93×74.5)

'In painting a landscape', said Matisse to his students in 1908, 'you choose it for certain beauties – spots of colour, suggestions of composition. Close your eyes and visualize the picture; then go to work, always keeping these characteristics the important features of the picture ... Nature excites the imagination to representation. But one must add to this the spirit of the landscape ... Your composition should indicate the more or less entire character of these trees, even though the exact number you have chosen would not accurately describe the landscape.' Nearly forty years later he wrote: 'There is an inherent truth which must be disengaged from the outward appearance of the object represented. This is the only truth that matters.' The painting here reproduced shows how perfectly he has followed his own precepts. His subject was trees growing round the margin of a pool. No doubt there were more trees than the picture shows, more branches and twigs upon those represented, a vast tangle of phenomena, irrelevant to Matisse's intentions. Yet he has selected precisely what he required, sufficient to make luminously clear to the beholder the lineaments of the place he chose to paint, as well as its spirit. From the profusion of nature as it must have appeared to him as he stood beside the pool Matisse has disengaged the 'inherent truth' about it. This is not simply its key features, but its essence and his response to it. The procedure that Matisse recommended, and followed, is the precise opposite from that urged upon beginners by Ruskin 'to go to nature ... rejecting nothing, selecting nothing'.

This painting is one of several, all of trees, made in 1916 and the following year, around the little pond of Trivaux, which lies a couple of miles south-west of Matisse's house on the route de Clamart, near Paris.

PAUL KLEE 1879–1940
A Girl's Adventure 1922
Water-colour 17$^{1}/_{4}$×12$^{5}/_{8}$ (44×32)

Klee is one of the most fascinating artists of the twentieth century. He has been dead for only twenty-two years; yet already writers all over the world have tried to solve the enigma of the immensely various and complex world of his creation. Many influences are traceable in his work, and he was at pains to elucidate his ideas in sundry writings, yet his art eludes – to a greater degree perhaps than that of any of his contemporaries – critical explanation. Yet it is not difficult to enjoy, for it is an expression of lyrical intimate rhythms and fantasies to which we may readily respond without precisely comprehending. Lovers of art are no longer disposed to regard his work as the charming irresponsible 'doodles' of a sophisticated adult with the knack for exploiting naïve qualities in children's drawings, for it is now generally recognized that Klee was a man of subtle and penetrating, although often obscure, ideas and intuitions and of extreme sensibility. He himself had a high sense of his personal calling as an artist. 'I cannot be understood in purely earthly terms,' he wrote, 'for I can live with the dead as with the unborn. Somewhat nearer to the heart of all Creation than is usual. But still far from being near enough.' For all its seriousness there was nothing solemn about his art, which abounds in the most delicate imagery, wit and humour. Modern art has produced no figure more various in invention than he, and few more meticulous and ingenious technicians.

The picture here reproduced is one of four belonging to the Tate. With two of the others it was bought from the first officially sponsored exhibition of the work of Klee in Great Britain, which was arranged by the Tate at the National Gallery in 1945, at a time when its own building had been rendered unfit for exhibition purposes by bombs.

MAX ERNST b. 1891
Lel hommes n'en sauront rien 1923
Canvas 31⁵/₈×25¹/₈ (80.5×64)

This painting, regarded by many as one of Ernst's outstanding works of
the surrealist period, has this commentary on the back in the form of a
prose poem:

LES HOMMES N'EN SAURONT RIEN

Le croissant (jaune et parachute) empêche que le petit sifflet tombe par
terre. Celui-ci, parce qu'on s'occupe de lui, s'imagine monter au soleil.
Le soleil est divisé en deux pour mieux tourner.
Le modèle est étendu dans une pose de rêve. La jambe droite est repliée
(mouvement agréable et exact).
La main cache la terre. Par ce mouvement la terre prend l'importance
d'un sexe.
La lune parcourt à toute vitesse ses phases et éclipses.
Le tableau est curieux par sa symmétrie. Les deux sexes se font équilibre.

The theme of the painting as of the poem is the correspondence between
sexual relations and the phases of the moon. A hand covers the earth with
the same protective gesture as that of the Venus Pudica. The Freudian
elaboration of its eroticism may owe something to the influence of Breton,
who had trained as a psycho-analyst.

Although it is a fully surrealist picture it was in fact painted during the
year preceding the promulgation of Breton's Surrealist Manifesto.

OSCAR KOKOSCHKA b. 1886
Polperro, Cornwall 1939–40
Canvas 23⁷/₈×34 (60.5×86.5)

Kokoschka is the most turbulent figure among living painters, a constitution-
al 'outsider'. This characteristic was no doubt exacerbated by the treatment he received in Vienna at a formative moment in his life. At the age
of twenty-two he was invited to participate in an important exhibition.
Certain of his contributions were virulently attacked, and he was dismissed
from the School of Arts and Crafts where he was a student. As a consequence the notorious and persecuted youth was championed by the progressive intellectual and artistic elements in Vienna, and from this time
forward he has consistently identified himself with 'the Opposition'. His
temperamental turbulence was fostered by the more bracing intellectual
climate of Berlin, in particular by the impact of the Expressionist movement. Kokoschka was an Expressionist born, but the influence of such
leaders of the movement as Nolde, Heckel, Pechstein and Kirchner power-
fully confirmed his own innate predilections. The Expressionists' aim which
was in closest accord with the needs of his own temperament was the
formation of a method of painting that would convey spiritual and emotional experience with an immediacy and a force that the elaborations of
traditional painting obstructed.

Kokoschka's restless spirit has driven him to many different parts of the
world, and in 1938, since he had become a prominent critic of the Nazis,
to England, where he lived continuously for some ten years and has lived
intermittently since and become a British subject. But in an England at war
against his enemies his turbulence had meagre scope, and it must be admitted that his adopted country has shown little disposition to honour a
man who had for more than half a century been a European celebrity as a
painter of rare endowments and rare courage.

The painter spent nine months, from the autumn of 1939 until the summer
of 1940, in Polperro, Cornwall, living in a fisherman's cottage. The picture
here reproduced was painted in this cottage and it represents the view from
an upper window. Another version is in a private collection in London.
Polperro, Cornwall was presented to the Tate by Dr Benés, President of
Czechoslovakia, when his Government was in exile in London, in 1941.

The Gallery also possesses a *Portrait of Ivan Maisky,* the wartime Am-
bassador of the Soviet Union, in London.

170

GEORGES BRAQUE b. 1882
Guitare et Pichet 1927
Canvas $31^7/_8 \times 45^1/_8$ (81 × 116.5)

Braque might have been describing his own course when he wrote that 'in art, progress does not consist in extension, but in the knowledge of limits'. 'In my own painting,' he said, with his perfect self-knowledge, 'I return continually to the centre ... I always try to have a focal area of great intensity, I concentrate things.' He is not a painter of great range, like

172

Picasso, or like Rouault, of tragic insight, or an ingenious wit like Klee; he is that rare being, the pure painter. Having no message to communicate he wisely confines his subjects to still-life, and no painter of his time has evoked from the contemplation of ordinary things—bread, stoves, fruit, packets of cigarettes—so gravely beautiful or so various a poetry.

JOAN MIRO b. 1893
Femmes, Oiseau au Clair de Lune 1949
Canvas 32×26 (81.5×66)

The painting of the twentieth century is enveloped in an aura of solemnity. Fauvism is vehement, Cubism sombre, Expressionism hysterical and tinged with self-pity, Surrealism melodramatic, Abstraction hygienic, Realism for ever peering with jaundiced eye into the kitchen sink. To all these movements belongs the credit of impressive achievement, but not even the most fervent of their admirers attribute to these achievements a spark of wit or humour. Indeed it would be out of harmony with the mystique of 'art appreciation' that is today's substitute for enjoyment to look for such qualities as wit or humour in an admired example of modern art. The pundits have made it plain that art is no laughing matter, and not to keep a perfectly straight face in its presence is a breach of taste. There are a few painters, however, in whose art wit or humour do play an integral part. There is much of both, for instance, in many of the works of Klee, and lest there should be any misapprehension on this point Klee's titles are there to put it right. One of his etchings is significantly entitled *Perseus, the Triumph of Wit over Suffering!* Miró is genuinely a painter: he has at his command an hallucinatory sense of colour and space and an expressive sinuosity of line. None the less wit and humour are no less conspicuous in his art, in which they assume a form even more fantastic though less spiritual or intellectual than in that of Klee. The art of Miró—unfashionable as it is to say so—is simple fun expressed with audacious fantasy and elegant sophistication.

ALBERTO GIACOMETTI b. 1901
Seated Man 1949
Oil on canvas 31$^{1}/_{2}$×21$^{1}/_{4}$ (80×54)

This painting, like so many of Giacometti's male portraits, represents his brother Diego. It was, incidentally, among the first of his paintings to be bought for a public collection, and very shortly after its completion.

The paintings of Giacometti have the look of summary sketches and the figures the look of ghosts, yet they are made with infinite labour, and they continue to live in the memory long after more highly wrought pictures representing more substantial idiosyncratic subjects have been forgotten. If his figures are intangible and remote, the surrounding space has a positive character for which it is difficult to find a parallel in the art of any of Giacometti's contemporaries.

The art of Giacometti is marked by a curious ambiguity: his sculptures are virtually without volume and his paintings without colour. It is perhaps for this reason that his sculpture is admired more by painters than by sculptors and his painting more by sculptors than by painters.

JACKSON POLLOCK 1912–1956
Painting 1952
Duco on canvas 56¹/₂×75 (143.5×190.5)

This painting, a characteristic late work, is the Gallery's most important product of the highly influential New York School which emerged after the war.

At first sight it appears to be a random aggregation of trails of black paint with fortuitous areas of yellow and crimson. Accident played a crucial part in the later works of Pollock but it was not, as some of his many followers have supposed, to the detriment of their own work, pure accident, but accident within a system regulated by the painter's will.

This painting was begun with the pouring of black and coloured paints over the canvas which was laid on the floor; the canvas was then stood upright and more paint was applied and worked and trickled over the surface. An informed critic has remarked on the interplay of paint applied to the horizontal and that applied to the upright surface as a remarkable development out of the original drip paintings in which the paint was poured on to a horizontal surface. It is more remarkable still as the product of the interplay between calculation and accident.

Like all Pollock's later and most characteristic work, *Painting 1952* is a total repudiation of traditional values in terms of a highly personal 'action'.

FERNAND LEGER 1881–1955
Two Women holding Flowers 1954
Canvas 38¼×51⅛ (97×130)

This work belongs to a series of paintings and preparatory studies in gouache or pen-and-ink known as *The Country Outing*, begun about 1943 and culminating in 1954 in the large final painting which as it were sums up the series and carries its title, although the artist made a few paintings on the same theme in 1955, the year of his death.

Two Women holding Flowers worthily represents the last phase of Léger's work when he had won, with a lifetime's struggle, an ultimate lucidity of expression and serenity of spirit.

MODERN SCULPTURE

ALFRED STEVENS 1817–75
Valour and Cowardice c. 1860
Plaster 103$^{1}/_{2}$ (263)

The work here reproduced is the full-scale plaster model for one of the two great bronze sculptures which form part of the Wellington Monument in St Paul's Cathedral.

The story of the monument is a tragedy; indeed the whole history of art scarcely affords an example so extreme, so unredeemed, of official persecution of a great sculptor officially commissioned. At a moment when British sculpture was at its lowest, after many changes and chances, Stevens was grudgingly adjudged the winner of the competition, open to sculptors of all nations, held in 1856 for the erection of a monument to the Duke of Wellington. It was by a miracle that at such a moment the services of a sculptor not unworthy of his Renaissance precursors should have been available to the authorities. The Dean of St Paul's regarded the monument as 'an encumbrance'. Mr Ayrton, First Commissioner of Works (whose face is the face of 'Falsehood' in the companion bronze), at one moment had Stevens' models impounded and his studio boarded up. The harassed artist was driven to his death with his work incomplete. In 1899 MacColl (seven years later to become the Tate's second Keeper) discovered in the crypt of St Paul's the plaster cast for the monument's crowning feature, the equestrian figure, headless, with the tail and a hoof of the horse missing, and he took the initiative in a campaign for the completion of the monument, which only came to pass some thirty-seven years after the sculptor's death.

The vehemence of the twentieth-century recoil from the false classical has blinded the eyes of this, in general, most appreciative of all ages to the genuine classical when it does appear, especially out of mid-Victorian England. This splendid monument still awaits due recognition. Recognition here and there it has received. 'It is', wrote the poet and scholar Laurence Binyon, 'already a classic; one of those complete and fruitful creations to which the *magnum incrementum* of Virgil's phrase will come in the enrichment it will give to other minds in later generations, and, through them, to other works of differing beauty.'

GEORGE FREDERIC WATTS 1817–1904
Clytie c. 1868–80
Bronze 33 (84)

It was primarily as a sculptor that Watts received his sketchy early training, and from his boyhood he had an ardent love for the Elgin Marbles. By far the larger part of his immensely productive life was given to painting, but he retained something of a sculptor's feeling and towards 1860 it strongly asserted itself. Of the various sculptures he made, that here reproduced is probably the finest. It will not bear comparison with a bust by Rodin, but considering how poor is the English sculptural tradition of the nineteenth century and that Watts himself came late to sculpture, it is impressive indeed. The dramatic pose is expressed with a burning energy and an understanding of solid form, both qualities very rarely encountered – except in the work of Stevens – in the sculpture of Watts' English contemporaries. It is indicative of his feeling for sculpture that, at a time when sculptors' works in marble were executed by assistants, Watts carved the original marble version of *Clytie* himself. (This was made in 1868; a number of bronze casts, of which the Tate's version is one, were made later from a clay model.)

According to the artist's widow, *Clytie* was inspired by a model named 'Long Mary', but the muscles were carefully studied from a well-known Italian male model named Colorossi, and other parts of the bust from the three-year-old daughter of Burne-Jones, observed in her mother's arms. 'I much desire your good opinion of my bust', Watts wrote to Gladstone, 'and must explain that my aim in this my first essay has been to get flexibility, impression of colour, and largeness of character, rather than purity and gravity – qualities I own to be extremely necessary to sculpture, but which, being made, as it seems to me, exclusively the objects of the modern sculptor, have deadened his senses to some other qualities making part – often glories – of ancient Art, and this has resulted in bare and cold work.' Of *Clytie* the young Swinburne, just down from Oxford, wrote, 'Not imitative, not even assimilative of Michael Angelo's manner it yet by some vague and ineffable quality brings to mind his work rather than any Greek sculptor's. There is the same intense and fiery sentiment, the same grandeur of device, the same mystery of tragedy.'

AUGUSTE RODIN 1840–1917
St John the Baptist Preaching 1879–80
Bronze 78³/₄ (200)

The slander that his *Age of Bronze* was simply a cast from his model rankled and Rodin was determined to answer it by modelling a figure over life-size. Two Italians knocked one day at his door: one a model who had already posed for him; the other, a wild-looking peasant named Pignatelli, just arrived from his native Abbruzzi, who had never posed. Taking off his clothes Pignatelli mounted the model stand, where with head thrown back, talking with passionate gestures as though haranguing a mob, he advanced towards the sculptor, who told him to hold his pose, and set immediately to work on a sketch half the size of the final figure of *St John the Baptist Preaching*–his third major work. The figure had originally a shepherd's crook in his left hand. The sculpture, when it was shown in the Salon of 1880, had only a modest success, but the model–who also sat to Rodin for *The Thinker, Ugolino* and a number of other figures–was enormously admired and thereafter in constant demand. Rodin modelled his *St John*, like his *Age of Bronze*, in the early morning and late at night, for during the day he was occupied as a drudge in the shop of a tradesman-sculptor.

'Rodin's subject is not the model', in the percipient words of a former Keeper of the Tate, 'demonstrating his own pattern in a pose emptied of all other purpose ... it is the various animal man, instrument primeval and perpetual of impulses that set the limbs dancing in the woods, cramp them in threatening tension, relax them in the oblivion of sleep or torment them in wild embraces.'

The *St John* was the first work by Rodin to come into British national possession, being purchased by public subscription in 1902.

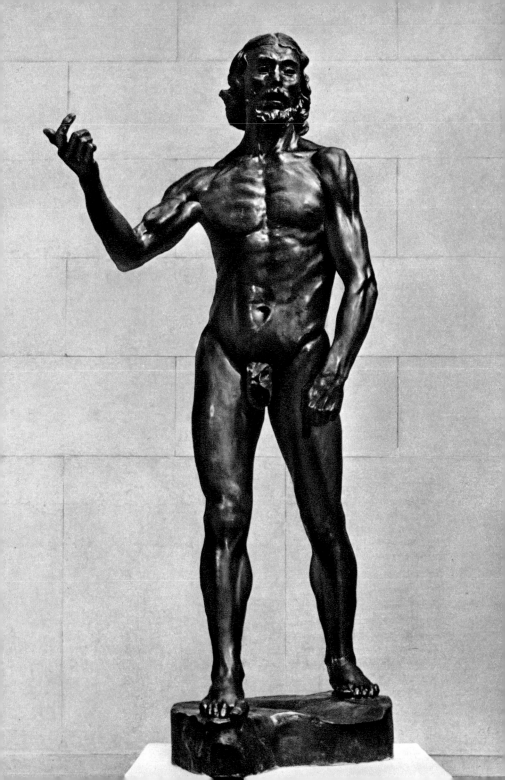

AUGUSTE RODIN 1840–1917
The Muse c. 1896
Bronze 57 (145)

The great monumental sculptor is a rare phenomenon in the modern world; rarer still is the patron able to make the fullest use of his genius. The history of most of the important monuments projected during the nineteenth and twentieth centuries is a history mainly of frustration and unrealized hope. In this respect the history of the monument of which the sculpture here reproduced was designed to form part is no exception.

Rodin was commissioned in 1889 to make for the Pantheon a monument to Victor Hugo. He first modelled the poet seated with three entwined sea-nymphs whom he eventually replaced by two other female figures, one of which was *The Muse of Meditation*, known later simply as *The Muse*, standing beside the poet, in the words of one of Rodin's biographers, 'enfolded in dreams and surrounding him with the calm ecstasy of meditation'. The authorities appear to have been shocked by the nudity of the poet and his muses, which seemed to them unsuitable for the Pantheon. After two years of wrangling Rodin was authorized to carry out the seated figure of Hugo alone, in marble, for the Luxembourg Gardens, and commissioned to make a standing figure, conventionally dressed, for the Pantheon. Rodin was once asked why he left *The Muse* incomplete. 'My figure', he replied, 'represents Meditation; that's why it has neither arms to act nor legs to walk. Haven't you noticed that reflection, when persisted in, suggests so many plausible arguments for opposite decisions that it ends in inertia?'

Detached though it is from the rest of the projected monument, *The Muse* is among the most splendid of Rodin's figures, an embodiment of relaxed energy.

AUGUSTE RODIN 1840–1917
The Age of Bronze 1875–7
Bronze 71¼ (181)

Today Rodin is acknowledged as the greatest sculptor of the modern world. When he made the bronze here reproduced – his second major work – he was entirely unknown; indeed he undertook it in the hope that it would establish his reputation in Paris. His original idea, drawn perhaps from the recent defeat of France, was that it should represent a defeated figure, and he called it *The Conquered*, and under this title it was first shown in Brussels, where it was modelled. Later on, however, it seemed to the sculptor to have assumed a character of its own which demanded the title of *Man awakening to Nature*, and finally *The Age of Bronze*, titles suggested to him perhaps by his own wanderings in the country and the nature-worship of Jean-Jacques Rousseau, a writer for whom he had a particular admiration. The figure does indeed appear to represent a young man at the moment of awakening to consciousness of being.

For this figure Rodin wanted as a model a man who had not been spoiled by having to take the conventional poses required of professionals, and he eventually found a handsome young army telegraphist named Auguste Neyt. At this figure (of which the left hand originally held a staff – perhaps to support the model during his endless posing) Rodin worked strenuously for eighteen months. In 1877 the plaster was shown in Brussels, where it was treated with derision, and in the Paris Salon the same year, where it provoked an extraordinary incident. The sculptor had modelled the figure with such subtle understanding that he was accused of having cast it from moulds taken directly from the body of the model. Against this accusation of fraud he defended himself by supplying photographs of a cast made in such a way, but his evidence was ignored.

The incident caused him acute distress, but it was testimony from his enemies to his understanding of the human body and no sculptor of any age has understood it more profoundly. By way of making amends to the sculptor the State purchased, three years later, the bronze cast, paying him no more than the cost of the casting. This was placed in the Luxembourg Gardens; it was believed that the authorities were afraid to show it in the Luxembourg Museum.

AUGUSTE RODIN 1840–1917
Cybele c. 1904–5
Bronze 63¹/₂ (161.5)

There is some doubt when this heroic twice life-size figure of the Mother
of the Gods was modelled. The year 1889 has been mentioned, but its style
suggests that it may date from some time not long before it was first shown,
in plaster, as *Torse de Femme* at the Salon in 1905. It has the extraordinary
freedom of modelling characteristic of the later work of Rodin, when
having wrested his unique knowledge of the human figure from unremitting
effort he was able to compose with the elements he had come to know so
well, to suggest, in particular, the outward thrusts of bone and muscle
against the skin. The figure was modelled from Abruzzezzi, who also sat
to Rodin for a number of figures for his *Hell Gate*, the grandiose project
that had occupied him at intervals since about 1880. No work better ex-
emplifies the noble simplicity for which Rodin was ever seeking, or the
surging energy which, even as with *Cybele* when the figure is in repose, is
the supreme characteristic of his art. The Tate's bronze, strangely enough,
is the only one known. It is an enlargement made from an earlier half life-
size study, made perhaps in 1889. Together with *The Age of Bronze* and
sixteen other sculptures *Cybele* was presented in 1914 to the British nation
–for which he had a particular affection–by Rodin himself.

EDGAR DEGAS 1834–1917
The Little Dancer Aged Fourteen 1880–1
Bronze 39 (99)

Because the statue here reproduced has become so familiar, its strangeness, indeed its uniqueness, is often overlooked. There is, in fact, nothing like it in the whole history of sculpture. It is a fitting memorial to its creator's strange and obscure life as a sculptor. This statue, shown at the Impressionist exhibition of 1881, was the only example of his sculpture to be seen during his life by the public. When he died about a hundred and fifty pieces of sculpture were found in his apartment – a mere fraction of his production – mostly wrecks of clay or wax covered with dust, many of them themselves crumbled into dust. Almost all artists, however reserved, are subject to the impulse to communicate, through their art, their ideas and their emotions. Where his paintings were concerned, Degas was clearly subject to it, but he was content to spend half a lifetime in the making of sculpture that – with this one exception – he never showed, nor even troubled to give permanent form by having it cast in bronze. (The seventy-four existing bronzes were all cast after his death.) Only a few friends were given the freedom of Degas' apartment, and little is known, even now, of the full range of the work of one of the great sculptors of the century.

Degas seems to have begun as a sculptor mainly with studies of horses, and it is not known when he first modelled the human figure. It was probably around 1879 that the little girl from the children's ballet class of the Opéra who is the subject of this bronze began to pose for Degas, but by way of leading up to the final figure in wax he made drawings of her both nude and dressed; he also modelled her nude. The innovations he made – innovations which would, incidentally, be treated with derision were not Degas an acknowledged master – in order to give his figure the look of startling realism at which he aimed were of the most audacious kind. *The Little Dancer* wore a real bodice, shoes, silk ribbon for her hair, her now famous *tutu*, and her skin was tinted. The whole was minutely finished, even down to the wrinkles in her stockings. The character of the angular little figure, not least of her impudent little face, and the pent-up energy and the beautiful abrupt rhythms of the taut pose give it a place among the supreme masterpieces of nineteenth-century sculpture.

ARISTIDE MAILLOL 1861–1944
Torso of the Monument to Blanqui c. 1905–6
Lead 47¹/₂ (120.5)

The Monument to Blanqui, a full-length striding female nude with her hands manacled behind her back, it at Puget-Théniers, near Grenoble.

Louis-Auguste Blanqui (1805–81) was a French revolutionary and socialist. It was decided to erect a monument to his memory in his birthplace, and a committee was formed, over which Clemenceau presided. When Maillol came before the committee he enquired who Blanqui was and how he had spent his life. It being explained to him that Blanqui, a champion of liberty, had been imprisoned for his principles, Maillol said simply, 'I will make you a beautiful nude woman, which will be *Liberty in Chains*.' For this reason it is sometimes known by this title, or else that of *Action in Chains*. It is for this statue that the Tate's *Torso* is a preliminary study. Apart, however, from the allusion to liberty in the title he suggested, Maillol paid little attention to the specific requirements of his commission; he was interested only in the pretext afforded him for making another likeness of the beautiful and vigorous body of his young wife, who also inspired a number of his other sculptures. The statue was disliked by the local authorities at Puget-Théniers and for some time it was kept covered up, and no record appears to have been kept of the date of its inauguration.

The *Torso* is a personification of energy and abundance: in comparison with it Maillol's other sculptures in the Gallery, *Venus with the Necklace*, of 1918–29, and *The Three Nymphs*, of c. 1930–8, for all their reticent beauty, seem to be lacking in life.

198

HENRI MATISSE 1869–1954
The Back I c. 1910–12
Bronze 74×45¹/₂ (188×115.5)

The over life-size bronze figure in relief here reproduced is the first of a series of four, the whole of which now belongs to the Tate. The series, which constitutes Matisse's largest work in sculpture, covers the span of the artist's development from his starting-point within the tradition of the nineteenth century to the simplification, radical and assured, which he eventually attained. Thus the series not only illuminates the progress of one of the great modern masters, but it also constitutes an epitome of one of the main developments of the art of the twentieth century.

The first of the series was shown, in plaster, at the Second Post-Impressionist Exhibition, held at the Grafton Galleries, London, in 1912, but the third and fourth remained unexhibited and almost unknown until they were shown in the retrospective exhibitions in Lucerne and Paris of 1949 and 1950. A further relief, which had never been out of the studio in which the artist had made it, was brought to light by his family a few months after his death. This is clearly the second of the series, and it fills what had been a wide stylistic gap between the first and what is now the third, so that the completed series of four now forms a majestic and regular procession from the comparatively naturalistic first state to the nearly abstract last one. The title under which the first was exhibited in London in 1912, *Le Dos, Plaster Sketch,* suggests that Matisse already intended to develop it further, and at intervals between that time and about 1930 he made the three other versions, all on the same scale. *Nu de Dos I* appears in the big painting, *The Painter's Studio*, of 1911. which is in the Museum of Modern Western Art, Moscow.

AMEDEO MODIGLIANI 1884–1920
Head c. 1913
Stone 24¹/₂ (63)

Modigliani was encouraged by Brancusi, in 1909, to try his hand at sculpture, which had been one of his early interests, but which he practised intermittently for only a few years. For sculpture as for painting it was a time of rapid change. The authority of the Greco-Roman tradition was in rapid decline, and sculptors were exposing themselves with enthusiasm to the influences emanating from the sculpture of the Ivory Coast, Egypt, India and China. In the sculpture of Modigliani these exotic influences are clearly perceptible, but its most conspicuous characteristic, elegance and extreme elongation, seems to belong innately to his own style. In the sculpture here reproduced its elongation, as well as its sharp-edged character, however, evidently owes much to the direct influence of African sculpture, but its contemporary qualities of elegance and sophistication are entirely his own.

In his lifetime Modigliani's talents as a sculptor received little encouragement. Mr Augustus John bought two heads of similar character from the artist himself. Modigliani was sometimes too poor even to buy his materials, and his friend and fellow sculptor Jacques Lipchitz remembers him carving a life-size caryatid from a building stone abandoned by workmen who had been called up for service in the First World War. Modigliani's death at thirty-six removed prematurely a painter-sculptor of the rarest talent.

The Tate Gallery also owns two fine examples of his painting, *Portrait of a Girl* and *The Little Peasant*, both of 1917.

HENRI GAUDIER-BRZESKA 1891–1915
Horace Brodzky 1913
Bronze 26³/₄ (68)

The history of sculpture during the twentieth century offers no stranger
phenomenon than the career of Gaudier-Brzeska. Without the advantage of
training and harassed always by extreme poverty he produced in a working
life of less than four years an astonishing quantity of work, much of it
worthy of a place among the finest sculpture and drawing of his time, before
his death at the age of twenty-four. He was born in France, the son of a
carpenter, of a family said to be descended from stone-cutters who had
carved some of the figures at Chartres Cathedral. The greater part of his
life was spent in England, which he first visited in 1906. He formed an
all-absorbing and enduring but troubled friendship with Sophie Brzeska,
a highly strung Polish woman who was twice his age when they first met
in 1910 and whose name he added to his own.

The working life of Gaudier-Brzeska was so brief and so erratic the
course of his progress, in which desperate need, vanity, the pressures of
fashion and sheer eccentric high spirits all played their part, that it is
difficult to discern the logical development of the essential elements in his
art. Before he had evolved a consistent style he was killed in action in his
native land, and his studio – half of Railway Arch 25, Putney – was pillaged,
and out in front of it the grass had grown up about the stones he had
planned to carve. In spite of the contradictory evidence of the surviving
work and of the artist's own pronouncements, there is reason for thinking
that by the time of his death he was feeling his way back towards a more
traditional approach. In a letter from the Front he suggested that he was
becoming gradually convinced that he had come to the end of his need for
research and that he intended to do more work of a more realistic kind.

The bronze here reproduced – one of the finest of all his sculptures –
shows the extraordinary combination of energy and economy that was
particularly his own. The effects of his sympathy with Cubism are clearly
apparent, but there are also intimations of his abiding love for Rodin, who,
he declared, was 'for France what Michelangelo was for Florence'.

PIERRE-AUGUSTE RENOIR 1841–1919
Venus Victrix 1914
Bronze 72 (183)

When Renoir began to make sculpture he was already an old man near the end of his life, with hands almost paralysed by rheumatism. It would seem that it was not even his own idea. 'If I have tried to make sculpture', he said, 'it isn't to annoy Michelangelo, nor because painting is not enough for me, but because Monsieur Vollard very gently compelled me.' Vollard, however, said that 'the demon of sculpture tempted Renoir'. Renoir had made a medallion and a bust of Coco, his youngest boy, the only two sculptures modelled entirely with his own crippled hands, when Vollard adroitly brought him in touch with a gifted young student of Maillol's named Richard Guino, and the association gradually aroused his interest in sculpture. 'Arriving at Renoir's', Vollard relates, 'I found him with a small lump of clay in front of him. "I can't resist it," he said, "I'm going to try a small figure."' This small figure was in fact a head which he was just able to model with wooden sticks, and for which under Renoir's guidance Guino made the body of a small Venus; eventually it was to grow into the great bronze here reproduced. Before setting Guino to work on this large version Renoir asked a friend to secure for his guidance the measurements of a Greek Venus, 'not the Venus de Milo', he said, 'who is a great policeman, but the Venus of Arles or the Venus de Medici'. With the aid of these measurements and of a local young woman called Maria for a model, Renoir developed the small original version, taking endless pains to attain a perfect fusion of naturalness and style. Unable himself to work the clay (which was dug from his own garden) he directed the operations of Guino. Vollard has described Renoir standing beneath his olive-trees at Cagnes, a long stick in his hand, tapping the clay to guide his assistant. This statue – the one, apart from the medallion and the head referred to, upon which he himself worked the most – is a serene embodiment of the style and naturalness at which he aimed.

PIERRE-AUGUSTE RENOIR 1841–1919
La Laveuse c. 1917–18
Bronze 48 (122)

The statue here reproduced is part of a project that remained incomplete on Renoir's death. This project was for two complementary statues, one a washerwoman, representing Water, the other a blacksmith, representing Fire. Several small preliminary studies in terracotta of both were made by Guino, his assistant, in 1916 from sketches by Renoir and under his supervision. Like *Venus Victrix, The Washerwoman* was made at Renoir's house at Cagnes, but without a model, and not in the garden under the olive-trees but in a small building intended for work in ceramic.

Relations between Renoir and Guino became strained, and in December 1918 they reached breaking-point, so that Renoir sought the intervention of two friends to ask Guino to discontinue work in progress. The project for the large *Blacksmith* was accordingly abandoned and the large *Washerwoman* remains without the final elaboration and refinement that Renoir would have given to it had he not been deprived by his now crippling infirmity even of the capacity to direct the efforts of others, or had he not dispensed with the services of an assistant deeply versed in all his procedures. Even in its unfinished state *The Washerwoman* is a beautiful and memorable work, and considering that Renoir made none of the preliminary studies in clay, and had no direct part in the large version, this is a wonderfully faithful reflection of the noble and radiant vision of the master.

CONSTANTIN BRANCUSI 1876–1957
Study for Mlle Pogany c. 1919–20
Bronze 11¹/₈ (28)

The first head of Mlle Pogany was made in 1913; other, more abstract versions were made in 1919, 1920, 1925 and 1931. That this version is only a study is suggested by the absence of hands and arms and the summary treatment of the neck. In all the other versions the influence of Modigliani is apparent in the swan-like neck and the head resting on the hands. The eyes, prominent in the original version, are scarcely indicated in those made later on.

Most of Brancusi's works in metal are highly polished, but three out of four casts – including that belonging to the Tate – are unpolished.

This is the only sculpture by Brancusi in a British public collection.

'Since the Gothic', wrote Henry Moore, 'European sculpture had become over-grown with moss, weeds – all sorts of surface excrescences which completely concealed shape. It has been Brancusi's special mission to get rid of this overgrowth, and to make us once more shape-conscious. To do this he has had to concentrate on very simple direct shapes, to keep his sculpture, as it were, one-cylindered, to refine and polish a single shape to a degree almost too precious. Brancusi's work, apart from its individual value, has been of historical importance in the development of contemporary sculpture. But it may now be no longer necessary to close down and restrict sculpture to the single (static) form unit. We can now begin to open out. To relate and combine together several forms of varied sizes, sections and directions into one organic whole . . .'

SIR JACOB EPSTEIN 1880–1959
Jacob Kramer 1921
Bronze 25 (63.5)

For many years the figure sculpture of Epstein was the object of virulent attack. The sculptor himself was repeatedly provoked and spoke forcibly, sometimes with bitterness, in defence of his work. He was a man very confident in his own gifts, and he did not hesitate to express his confidence; perhaps attack provoked him to self-assertion. Until late in life, when he became something of a benevolent patriarch, he was widely regarded as an arrogant, opinionated man. For anyone to allow his reputation in this regard to affect his judgment of Epstein's sculpture, in particular his portrait busts, would be to invite serious error. For as an interpreter of human character his greatest quality was his receptivity. An account which he gave of his procedure bears the stamp of truth. 'In my portraits it is assumed', he wrote, 'that I start out with a definite conception of my sitter's character. On the contrary, I have no such conception in the beginning. My aim, to start with, is purely constructive. With scientific precision I make a quite coldly thought out construction of the form, giving the bony formations round the eyes, the ridge of the nose, mouth and cheekbones, and defining the relation of the different parts of the skull to each other. As the work proceeds I note the expression ... and the character of the model begins to impose itself ... In the end, by a natural process of observation, the mental and physiological characteristics impose themselves on the clay.' On the psychological level he was not, of course, unselectively receptive. It was the dramatic and dynamic elements, and also the exotic, that he was predisposed to receive and to reinterpret with the great resources he had at his disposal. Like many artists, he made his best portraits of those whom he invited to sit. Of these surely one of the finest is the head here reproduced of Jacob Kramer, the Leeds painter.

SIR JACOB EPSTEIN 1880–1959
The Visitation 1926
Bronze 65 (165)

The statue here reproduced was intended by the sculptor to be completed by the addition of a second figure; these were to represent *The Visitation*. It was modelled in clay in a little hut in Epping Forest. The sculptor recalled with pleasure how it looked in this little hut, and he would have liked it to stand in the open, among trees. It was intended to express humility or charity. The position which it occupies in the Tate can be missed by those entering the Gallery, but must be discovered by those leaving.

A curious feature of the figure sculpture of Epstein is the marked contrast in character between those he has modelled and those he has carved: the two methods foster different aspects of his art. The carved figures, for example *Night* and *Day*, on the Headquarters of the London Underground Railway, *Genesis, Behold the Man* and *Adam*, show him as a man in harmony with the prevailing tendency towards extreme distortion in the interests either of expression or of design. The modelled figures show him as a far more traditional, although certainly a no less individual artist, who allowed his subjects to impose their own character upon him. *The Visitation*, a nobly expressive figure, has a high place among his modellings. It is the only life-size figure by Epstein in the Tate, which possesses, however, *The Rock Drill* and no less than ten of his portrait busts as well as two of his drawings.

FRANK DOBSON b. 1888
Sir Osbert Sitwell, Bt. 1923
Brass 12¹/₂ (32)

The maker of the sculpture here reproduced suffers in reputation today
for having been earlier misunderstood and on that account extravagantly
praised. When at the end of the First World War he emerged as a figure
to be reckoned with – he had started as a painter and had made his first
carving only about a year before the war began – he was mistaken for an
innovator. To be *different* from a predecessor – a recent predecessor at all
events – was to be *better* than he: that was the prevailing notion. In a preface
to a book on Dobson a well-known critic explained that 'all the accom-
plishment of Rodin' could not conceal the 'formal inadequacy' of his work,
but that Dobson was 'one of the three most interesting living sculptors in
the world', and the best that England had produced 'for about six hundred
years'. The fact was that Dobson was not an innovator at all. His work,
as the same critic noted, showed that he had looked at African and Asian
sculpture and was interested in abstract form. In this, however, his preoccupations were identical with those of almost all the thinking artists of
his generation: his art was quite simply and naturally derived from the
leading innovating painters and sculptors at work before the war, in Paris:
Picasso, Modigliani, Brancusi; in London: Wyndham Lewis, Gaudier-Brzeska
and other Vorticists. Dobson is a man with a strong natural sculptural sense,
assiduously cultivated, who has been content to accept the ideas which have
prevailed during his own formative years. What admirable use he could
make of such ideas is manifest in the taut, closely knit forms of this fine
head, *Sir Osbert Sitwell*: a searching likeness expressed in harmonious
form. It was bought from the sculptor by Lawrence of Arabia and lent by
him to the Tate and afterwards presented in accordance with his wishes
by his executors.

PABLO PICASSO b. 1881
Le Coq 1932
Bronze 25³/₈ (65)

It is a curious fact, symptomatic, perhaps, of the relative disinterest in sculpture in comparison with painting, that the sculpture of Picasso attracts such relatively little notice. The news of a mere scribble, let alone a new painting, by Picasso can arouse a flutter of excitement, but there must be many people familiar with other aspects of his work who would be surprised to learn that he is a prolific sculptor (more than two hundred examples were reproduced in a book on the subject published some ten years ago). His development as an artist has not been expressed continuously in his sculpture as it has in his painting, nor can he be called a great modeller, but he has made sculpture from at least as early as 1899, some of it of outstanding ingenuity and energy. There can be little modern sculpture to manifest a more spontaneous response to its subject, or on occasion such lively humour, as the sculpture of Picasso. It is of the most varying character: in 1929, for example, he even planned gigantic houses in the form of women's heads, to be built on the Mediterranean shore, which he was compelled, however, to paint, as no one was willing to commission such bizarre sculptures on such a scale. The earlier sculpture resembles his painting, whereas the later is more independent.

Le Coq was modelled at Picasso's Château of Boisegeloup, near Gisors, in the stables which he made into a studio for sculpture. Nothing could better illustrate the variety of his sculpture than the contrast between the bronze here reproduced and the almost abstract treatment of the same subject in wrought-iron only two years before.

Unlike most sculptors Picasso usually models directly in plaster rather than in clay.

HENRY MOORE b. 1898
Recumbent Figure 1938
Stone 35 (89)

In nothing do artists differ more than in the number of themes which pre-occupy them. The number of themes which have challenged the constant inventiveness of, say, Klee and Picasso is almost beyond counting. But there are artists of a different order who in the whole course if their lives are obsessed by but a few themes, and it is to this order that Moore conspicuously belongs. He is an artist of exceptional learning, and the evidence of his ardent admirations – for the sculpture of ancient Mexico, the primitive sculpture of Africa and Oceania, for Giotto, Masaccio and Picasso, to name but a few among many – is plainly manifest in his work. Yet if certain derivative sculptures belonging to his early years are excluded, the work of Moore shows an extraordinarily consistent effort to give form to a very few basic concepts. Massive nobility in repose and the dominant forms and rhythms of nature, for instance, are permanent features of his slowly evolving art. His concern, incidentally, with this aspect of nature has been widely misunderstood, and he has been represented as possessed by a scientist's interest in discovering her underlying forms and rhythms. This is absurd, simply because there is nothing mysterious about such forms and rhythms. A reliable treatise upon rocks or bones gives these particulars about them in the minutest detail. Moore is not ignorant of the existence of such treatises, and there is no evidence in his work that he has copied the authoritative diagrams they contain. It is evident, then, that he must be doing something different from research. It is not easy to define in words just what Moore is after, but someone writing about him quoted these words by Thomas Hardy, which, he perceptively observed, fit the work of Moore:

'Nature is played out as a Beauty, but not as a mystery ... I don't want to see the original realities – as optical effects that is. I want to see the deeper reality underlying the scenic, the expression of what are sometimes called abstract imaginings.'

HENRY MOORE b. 1898
Family Group 1949
Bronze 60 (152.5)

In the note accompanying Moore's *Recumbent Figure* it was stated that this sculptor's work was slow in its evolution. But it has evolved – and widened in scope in the process. The late 'thirties and early 'forties were the years when it most noticeably changed direction. Although there were signs of change before its outbreak, the war was its principal cause. In the years before, Moore had been too deeply absorbed in his art to give much attention to people, but his wartime drawings of exhausted sleepers in the London shelters required an intense scrutiny of people that was a new exercise for Moore – a scrutiny of people, not as models, or as forms, but as human beings. This sudden heightened awareness, in circumstances so moving, added a humanism to his art which remained, to its vast enrichment, a permanent feature of it.

The Tate Gallery is fortunate in possessing, among its thirty-five works by Moore, two which splendidly exemplify the two contrasting stages in the development of his art: the *Recumbent Figure*, of 1938, already briefly discussed, and the bronze here reproduced, made eleven years later. Like the large majority of his earlier figures, the former is female, weighty and passive. The latter not only manifests the humanism which he gained from his experience in the shelters, but it includes a male figure. Following the success of his shelter drawings he was invited to make a series of drawings of miners. Although he came of a mining family he had never been down a pit, and the sight of men working at the coal face led to the addition of the gaunt male body to his repertory of forms.

The *Family Group*, with its compelling and various rhythms and its mysterious combination of remote grandeur with a warm humanity, is among the finest of Moore's sculptures.

There are three other casts. The original was commissioned for the Barclay School, Stevenage, and the design was adapted from a small *Family Group* which Moore had made in 1945.

MARINO MARINI b. 1901
Cavaliere 1947
Bronze 63¹/₂ (161.5)

In Italy the end of the Second World War was followed by a period of extraordinary and often brilliant activity in all the arts, but particularly in sculpture. Of the many talented sculptors who have emerged two are recognized abroad as among the finest of their generation. One of them is Marino Marini. His most characteristic works show an audacity that is contemporary, combined with a constant awareness of the great sculpture of the past, especially the sculpture of ancient China. The horse and rider is a subject which for more than twenty years has excited his faculties to function at their highest pitch. There is a marked difference between the horses and riders of the middle 'thirties and those of more recent date. The earlier are static, conventional and wilfully archaic. The later are possessed by a violent inner life: the movements of both horse and rider seem to be made at the prompting of anguish; physical in the case of the horses, mental in the case of their riders. This change is attributed by the sculptor to his having seen, during the war, terrified Lombard peasants fleeing on horse-back from aerial bombardment. The Tate Gallery is fortunate in possessing a bronze, specially cast, of what is perhaps the finest of Marini's horses and riders; also a fine ink and pastel drawing of a similar subject made the year after the bronze.

ALBERTO GIACOMETTI b. 1901
Man Pointing 1947
Bronze 70 (178)

'Among the several sins that I have been accused of committing', declared Picasso, 'none is more false than the one that I have, as the principal objective in my work, the spirit of research. When I paint, my object is to show what I have found and not what I am looking for.' This spirit of research, repudiated by Picasso, animates the life of Giacometti. 'Let me know how to make only one statue', he says, according to Sartre, 'and I will be able to make a thousand.' 'So long as he does not know this', continued Sartre, 'Giacometti is not interested in statues at all, only in sketches, in so far as they help him towards his goal.' He exhibits as little as is compatible with survival, and perpetually dissatisfied he smashes all the work in his studio and begins again.

At one moment in his life his research became particularly desperate. 'To my terror', runs one of his letters, 'the sculptures became smaller and smaller, they only had a likeness when small, yet their dimensions revolted me ... A large figure seemed to me untrue and a small one intolerable, and then often they became so very small that with only one touch of my knife they disappeared into dust.' (Into dust because he models in plaster.) But all this changed somewhat in 1945 when he discovered to his surprise, through drawing, that he was able to model figures which expressed what was in his mind if he made them long and slender. The figure here reproduced was one of the earliest and remains one of the finest of these elongated figures which express, with a kind of aloofness, the always distant prospect of a human being in a great space.

GIACOMO MANZU b. 1908
The Cardinal 1947–8
Bronze 20 (50.5)

The Italian sculptor who, with Marino Marini, has taken a principal place
among the younger generation of European sculptors is Giacomo Manzù.
It happens with singular frequency in many spheres of creative endeavour
that figures appear in contrasting pairs: among French painters Ingres and
Delacroix come immediately to mind; among English, Reynolds and Gainsborough. It would be presumptuous to attempt, in the case of two productive figures midway in their careers, to anticipate the verdict of posterity,
but what is evident is that Manzù and Marini are just such a contrasting
pair. The work of Manzù is tender where Marini's is tough; serene where
it is dynamic; suave where it is angular, and above all intensely religious
where it is sheerly anguished. At a time when religious art is mostly mere-
tricious and effete Manzù goes forward, making bronze after bronze, drawing after drawing, of religious subjects, with the modest assurance of a man
working within a living tradition. But his tenderness does not arise from
want of courage: during the war he modelled low reliefs in which the
Crucified Christ is watched – and in one case tormented – by a soldier wearing a German helmet. Not all his subjects are religious; they also include
adolescents and romantic, tenderly sensual women.

The seated cardinal is a subject that has engaged Manzù ever since 1937.
The example here reproduced, like almost all his sculptures, is unique, and
the original plaster model has been destroyed.

The Tate also possesses another bronze, *Susanna*, of 1942–52, a reclining
woman, and three ink and wash drawings, one of a cardinal and two
chosen from the entire series of about twenty made between 1937 and 1944
by way of preparation for the *Susanna*.

REGINALD BUTLER b. 1913
Girl 1953–4
Shell bronze 70 (178)

Butler practised as an architect from 1937 until 1950, and during the Second World War he worked as a blacksmith. It was not until 1944 that he turned to sculpture, and for many years no sculptor has made a serious reputation so quickly. In 1953 he won the first prize in the international competition for the monument to 'The Unknown Political Prisoner'. When his winning model was at the Tate Gallery (where the prize-winning entries and runners-up were exhibited), it was deliberately destroyed by a demonstrator. The ensuing fuss focused attention on the work of Butler, and its exceptional merits were recognized more promptly than would otherwise have been the case. The Tate had acquired its first example of his work from his first one-man exhibition held four years before, a large and almost abstract figure, *Woman 1949*, in forged iron, which both in conception and execution derives to some degree from his having been a blacksmith. The bronze here reproduced marks a change in a representational direction, but it shows the energy and tautness of his earlier works impressively combined with a humanity that is new. A man of excellent education, he is sceptical about theories. The empiricism of his outlook is expressed by one of his sayings: 'Looking for sculpture is like trying to find the hub of a wheel. Often when one thinks one has found the hub – one is still along a spoke! Often one runs right through the hub and out along another spoke!

'If you travel outwards along a spoke *away* from the hub you come towards the sterile world of the academic art systems: "realism", "non-figuration", "the museum fragment".

'Art which packs a punch is *always near the hub*: it is a fusion of a multitude of strands.'

BRITISH SCHOOL

16th Century Portrait of a Lady

16th Century Sir Henry Unton

Van Somer Lady Elizabeth Grey

16th Century The Cholmondeley Sisters

Mytens The First Duke of
Hamilton as a Boy

Kneller The Angel appearing to Tobit

Wright Sir Neil O'Neill
(The Irish Chieftain)

233

Hogarth The Six Servants of Hogarth

Hogarth Scene from the 'Beggars Opera'

Griffier View of Hampton Court Palace

Ramsay Portrait of a Man

Wootton Members of the Beaufort Hunt

Lambert A Hilly Landscape with a Cornfield

Scott Admiral Anson's Action off Cape Finisterre

Stubbs Mares and Foals in a Landscape

Wilson A Venetian Gentleman

Devis The James Family

Zoffany Charles Macklin as Shylock

Zoffany A Family Group in a Landscape

Gainsborough View of Dedham

Gainsborough The Baillie Family

Reynolds Suzanna Beckford

Reynolds The Age of Innocence

Gainsborough The Housema

Wilson Llyn-Y-Cau, Cader Idris

Copley The Death of Major Peirson

Romney The Beaumont Family

Romney A Lady in a Brown Dress

West Sir Thomas Beauchamp-Proctor Bt

Stuart Benjamin West P.R.A.

Hoppner Mrs Williams

Opie The Peasant's Family

Blake The Penance of Jane Shore in St Paul's Church

Blake The House of Death

Blake Newton

Blake Bathsheba at the Bath

Blake Nebuchadnezzar

Blake Hecate

Blake The Procession from Calvary

Blake Landscape near Felpham

Blake Elijah

Blake Pity

Blake The Four and Twenty Elders
casting their Crowns before the Divine Throne

Blake The Spiritual Form of Nelson
guiding Leviathan

Blake The Ghost of a Flea

Blake The Inscription over the Gate

Blake The Ascent of the Mountain
of Purgatory

Blake Satan smiting Job with Sore Boils

Morland Morning: Higglers preparing for Market

Barker of Bath Landscape near Bath

240

Turner Portrait of the Artist when Young

Turner Holy Family

Turner Aeneas with the Sibyl: Lake Avernus

Turner View on Clapham Common

Turner Tree Tops and Sky

Turner Willows beside Stream

Turner Windsor, from Lower Hope

Turner Sunset on the River

Turner A River, with Castle and a Village

Turner The Ford

Turner Windsor Castle, from the Meadows

Turner Newark Abbey

Turner A Wide Valley, with a Town and Spire

Turner The Thames near Windsor

Turner Frosty Morning

Turner Rome, the Arch of Titus and the Forum
Romanum, seen from the Colosseum

Turner The Bay of Baiae,
with Apollo and the Sibyl

Turner George IV at a Banquet in Edinburgh

Turner Shipping off a Headland

Turner Music Party, Petworth

243

Turner Between Decks

Turner Yacht Racing in the Solent

Turner Watteau Painting *or* Watteau,
Study by Fresnoy's Rules

Turner A Ship aground

Turner Tivoli *or* Tobias and the Angel

Turner Childe Harold's Pilgrimage: Italy

Turner Sunrise: a Castle on a Bay

244

Turner Van Tromp returning after the Battle
off the Dogger Bank

Turner Interior at Petworth

Turner Norham Castle, Sunrise

Turner Phryne going to the Public Baths as
Venus: Demosthenes taunted by Aeschines

Turner The Thames from above Waterloo Bridge

Turner Procession of Boats with Distant Smoke, Venice

Turner Heidelberg Castle in the Olden Time

Turner Peace: Burial at Sea (detail)

Turner Venice: the Dogana, San Giorgio Maggiore,
Le Zitelle from the Steps of the Europa

Turner The Opening of the Walhalla, 1843:
Honour to King Ludwig the First of Bavaria

Turner Whalers

Turner Whalers (boiling Blubber) entangled
in Flaw Ice, endeavouring to extricate themselves

Raeburn The First Viscount Melville

Constable Mrs Andrew

Constable Flatford Mill

Constable View at Epsom

onstable Hadleigh Castle: the Mouth of the Thames

Richmond Christ and the Woman of Samaria

Crome Moonrise on the Yare (?)

Crome Mousehold Heath, Norwich

Etty Hero and Leander

Etty Britomart redeems Fair Amoret

Palmer The Bright Cloud

Wilkie Peep-O-Day Boy's Cabin: West of Ireland

Keene Self-portrait

Deverell The Pet

Millais The Order of Release, 1746

Millais Ophelia

Holman Hunt Strayed Sheep

Brett Glacier of Rosenlaui

Calderon Broken Vows

Ford Madox Brown Jesus washing Peter's feet

Ford Madox Brown Chaucer at the Court of Edward III

Wallis The Death of Chatterton

Frith The Derby Day

Morris La Belle Iseult

Rossetti The Annunciation

Rossetti Beata Beatrix

Burne-Jones
nia von Bork, 1560

Burne-Jones King Cophetua
and the Beggar Maid

Conder Springtime

Fildes The Doctor

Bramley A Hopeless Dawn

Marlow Capriccio, St Paul's and a Venetian Canal

Rothenstein The Doll's House

251

Beardsley The Fat Woman

Beardsley Caprice

Sargent
Graham Robertson

Sargent Asher Wertheimer

Orpen The Mirror

Steer Richmond Castle

John Miss Boughton-Leigh

Gertler The Artist's Mother

Ginner The Café Royal

William Nicholson Lowestoft Bowl

Gilman The Canal Bridge

Grant The Queen of Sheba

Gore The Gas Cooker

Gaudier-Brzeska Sophie Brzeska

253

Lewis Planners (Happy Day)

Gore From a Window in Cambrian Road, Richmond

Nevinson The Arrival

Nevinson La Mitrailleuse

Lucien Pissarro Ivy Cottage, Coldharbour

John Nash The Cornfield

Lamb Lytton Strachey

Roberts The Diners

Sickert Ennui

John Washing Day

John Joseph Hone

Sickert The Servant of Abraham

Tonks Mr Steer and Mr Sickert

Spencer The Apple Gatherers

Spencer Self-portrait

Spencer Christ carrying the Cross

Wadsworth Abstract Composition

Paul Nash Landscape from a Dream

Wadsworth The Beached Margin

M. Smith Cornish Church

M. Smith Model Turning

M. Smith Peonies

M. Smith Peaches

Coldstream Mrs Winifred Burger

Burra Mexican Church

Armstrong Coggeshall Church   *O'Conor* Still Life with Bottles   *Richards* Two Females

Moynihan The Teaching Staff of the Royal College   *Richards* Trafalgar Square, London
of Art

Bomberg Flowers   *Freud* Self-portrait

Sutherland
Somerset Maugham

Sutherland Head III

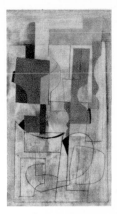

Ben Nicholson
Feb. 28 53 (vertical seconds)

Piper Three Suffolk Towers

Ben Nicholson White Relief

Lanyon Porthleven

Townsend Hop Alleys

Derrick Greaves Domes of Venice

Gross Gateway into Germany: the Maas in Flood
near the Berg Bridge

Gross Grey Landscape – Le Boulvé

Frost Khaki and Lemon

Nolan Glenrowan

Collins The Golden Wheel

J. Smith Bottles in Light and Shadow

Bratby Window, Self-portrait, Jean and Hands

Herman The Pit Pony

Colquhoun
Woman with Still Life

Hilton Grey Day by the Sea, February 1960

Heath Painting Brown and Black

Davie Entrance for a Red Temple No. 1

William Scott White Sand and Ochre

261

Bacon Reclining Woman

Bacon Seated Man with Turkey Rug

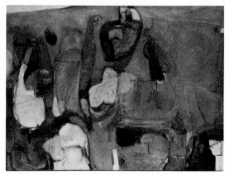

Whiteley Untitled Red Painting

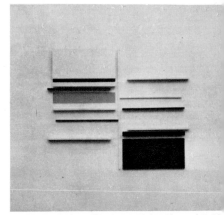

Pasmore Spiral Motif in Green, Violet, Blue and Gold

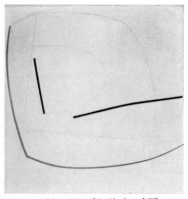

Pasmore Linear Motif in Black and White

Sisley The Bridge at Sèvres

Seurat Le Bec du Hoc, Grandchamp

Anquetin Girl reading a Newspaper

Monet Poplars on the Epte

Matisse Nude Study in Blue   *Matisse* André Derain   *Derain* Henri Matisse

Camille Pissarro Self-portrait   *Cézanne* The Gardener

Cézanne Still Life with Water Jug   *Cézanne* Mount Sainte Victoire

Delaunay The City

Kandinsky Schlacht (Battle)

Modigliani Portrait of a Girl

Metzinger Woman with a Coffee Pot

Vuillard The Laden Table

Dunoyer de Segonzac Still Life with a Cabbage

Moholy Nagy K VII

Soutine The Road up the Hill

Marin Downtown, New York City

Grosz Drawing for 'Der Speisser Spiegel'

Léger Leaves and Shell

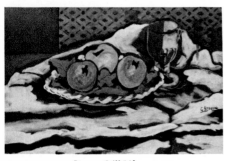

Braque Still Life

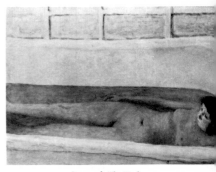

Bonnard The Bath

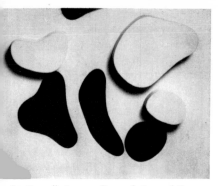

Arp Constellation according to the Laws of Chance

Chagall Bouquet with Flying Lovers

Rouault The Three Judges

Grüber Job

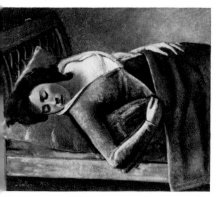

Balthus Sleeping Girl

Adler The Mutilated

Delvaux Venus Asleep

Morandi Still Life

de Staël Marathon

Picasso Seated Woman

Picasso Glass, Bottle and Guitar

Picasso Goat's Skull, Bottle and Candle

268

Manessier Minus 12°

Soulages 23 May 1953

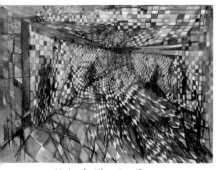

Vieira da Silva Grey Room

Dufy Deauville, Drying the Sails

Guston The Return

Guttuso The Discussion

Vasarely Nives II

Rothko Light Red over Black

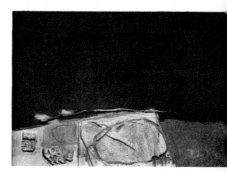

Appel Amorous Dance

Tapies Green and Grey Painting

MODERN SCULPTURE

Lipchitz Reclining Woman with Guitar

Laurens Woman Bathing

Maillol The Three Graces

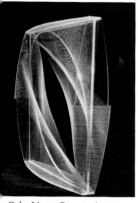

Gabo Linear Construction

Armitage People in a Wind

Richier Water

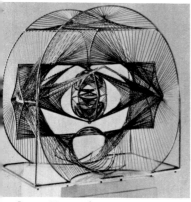

Pevsner Maquette for a Monument
symbolising the Liberation of the Spirit

Nimptsch Reclining Figure (Olympia)

271

Chadwick Winged Figures

Paolozzi Cyclops

Hepworth Figure (Nanji

Džamonja Metal Sculpture 14

Moore Figure

César The Man of Saint-Denis

Moore Two-piece Reclining Figure No. 2

LIST OF ILLUSTRATIONS

Page numbers in italic denote colour plates

275

278

284

TEXT REFERENCES TO THE INTRODUCTION

1. *The Times* 30 May 1851. 2. Ibid, 19 March and 1 April 1890. 3. Ibid, 21 June 1890. 4. 25 March 1890. 5. 23 June 1890. 6. 21 June 1890. 7. 29 June 1890. 8. 28 June 1890. 9. 26 July 1890. 10. 1 July 1890. 11. 16 and 28 July 1890. 12. *The Times* 22 July 1890. 13. House of Lords, 14 August 1890. 14. *The Times* 21 March 1891. 15. The correspondence was published in *The Times* 5 March 1892. 16. *Society* 20 February 1892. 17. 5 March 1892. 18. 19 March 1892. 19. 19 March 1892. 20. *The National Observer* 13 February 1892. 21. Sir Edward du Cane, 17 March 1892. 22. *The Daily News* 3 November 1892. 23. 29 November 1892. 24. *The Daily Mail* Interview with Tate, 8 May 1897. 25. 28 July 1897. 26. 22 July 1897. 27. *The Times* 12 May 1900. 28. *The Daily Chronicle* 12 May 1900. 29. I have given a fuller account of this collection in a Foreword to *The Works of Alfred Stevens in The Tate Gallery* by Kenneth Romney Towndrow 1950. 30. 5 September 1903. 31. 20 October 1903. 32. 'The Maladministration of the Chantrey Bequest' 25 April, and 'Parliament and the Chantrey Bequest' 6 June. 33. 13 and 22 May. 34 and 35. *Minutes of Evidence:* Q. and A. No. 479. 36. Ibid, 840. 37. Ibid, 842. 38. Ibid, 922. 39. Ibid, 925. 40. Ibid, 1476–7, 2265. 41. Ibid, Appendix I. 42. I have given a fuller account of this collection in a Foreword to *A Catalogue of the Works of William Blake in The Tate Gallery* by Martin Butlin 1957. 43. Minutes of the Meeting of the Board, 23 June 1930. 44. *Making, Knowing and Judging* 1956.

INDEX OF NAMES

286